The Bitcoin Investor

A Complete Guide to

Cryptocurrency Investing

Michael Gonzalez

Legal & Disclaimer

The information contained in this book and its contents is not designed to replace or take the place of any form of medical or professional advice; and is not meant to replace the need for independent medical, financial, legal or other professional advice or services, as may be required. The content and information in this book have been provided for educational and entertainment purposes only.

The content and information contained in this book have been compiled from sources deemed reliable, and it is accurate to the best of the Author's knowledge, information, and belief. However, the Author cannot guarantee its accuracy and validity and cannot be held liable for any errors and/or omissions. Further, changes are periodically made to this book as and when needed. Where appropriate and/or necessary, you must consult a professional (including but not limited to your doctor, attorney, financial advisor or such other professional advisor) before using any of the suggested remedies, techniques, or information in this book.

Upon using the contents and information contained in this book, you agree to hold harmless the Author from and against any damages, costs, and expenses, including any legal fees potentially resulting from the application of any of the information provided by this book. This disclaimer applies to any loss, damages or injury caused by the use and application, whether directly or indirectly, of any advice or information presented, whether for breach of contract, tort, negligence, personal injury, criminal intent, or under any other cause of action.

You agree to accept all risks of using the information presented inside this book.

You agree that by continuing to read this book, where appropriate and/or necessary, you shall consult a professional (including but not limited to your doctor, attorney, or financial advisor or such other advisor as needed) before using any of the suggested remedies, techniques, or information in this book.

You should never make an investment decision on an ICO or any other investment based on the information on this book, and you should never interpret or otherwise rely on any information on this book as an investment advice. Always consult a licensed investment advisor or other qualified financial professional if you are seeking investment advice on any ICO, cryptocurrency, currency, token sales, securities, or commodities.

Dedication

To all my friends at Crypto Cleveland who without their guidance, mentorship, and friendship none of this would be possible.

Preface

Welcome!

Okay, I know what you're thinking. "I'll just skip these first few pages and get to the real stuff."

Well, hold on. Just wait. This preface is a preparation for what you are about to read.

Actually, that's precisely what this book is all about — preparation and acting fast in the market. The ideas in these pages are revolutionary. I'm so glad this book is in your hands; it could save you from losing lots of money. This book has the potential to change the way you invest forever. Let me explain.

You see, when it comes to cryptocurrency investing, a lot of research and due diligence is genuinely needed. Although the cryptocurrency market has been in an extended bull run since its highs at the end of 2017, the opportunity to invest in the market has never been greater.

Currently, a significant problem when it comes to investing in cryptocurrencies is the lack of adequate resources out there to help beginners understand the market. When searching for crypto guides in the market, I couldn't find any definitive guides that go deep into cryptocurrency, mining, wallets, exchanges, private keys and more.

To help you better understand digital currencies, I have put together this comprehensive guide that features all you need to know about crypto. In these pages, you'll learn how blockchains work and about the top cryptocurrencies in the market. You will learn about the inherent risks involved with cryptocurrency investing as well as the secrets of profitable cryptocurrency investing.

This book will teach you how to start trading cryptocurrency, how to analyze coins, profitable ways of investing in crypto, and so much more. You'll never find a more intelligent, definitive and user-friendly crypto guide anywhere.

Once you dive into this book, I think there are two killer ways to read it: from front to back, and by picking and choosing the chapters you want to read. I truly hope you find this book as valuable as I intended to make it.

-Michael Gonzalez

Introduction

As you may already know, cryptocurrencies (crypto) have become one of the most significant topics of discussion in the technology sector since the Internet. While it may look like a new frontier to many people, businesses and governments have already recognized its potential. The hype around cryptocurrency is real.

Virtual currencies have captured our imagination, but the reality is that an overwhelming majority of people have a very limited understanding of cryptocurrencies. Even bankers, scientists, consultants, investors, and developers are still struggling to understand the basics of cryptocurrencies.

You may have heard of Bitcoin during the investigation of the illegal activities that were happening on the dark-web market called the Silk Road. After the Silk Road was shut down, a substantial amount of Bitcoin was confiscated and subsequently auctioned off by the U.S Marshals. Since then, Bitcoin has slowly emerged as an efficient way of transferring money over the Internet and as an investment asset.

In fact, in May 2010, when Bitcoin was worth a meager 0.08 USD, Laszlo Hanyecz posted on the Bitcoin forum that he had used 10,000 bitcoins to buy a couple of pizzas. Hanyecz is credited with making one of the first purchases of a good or service using Bitcoin. Today, those two pizzas he bought with Bitcoin are worth about 70 million USD (and counting).

As Bitcoin continues to gain legitimacy, its volatility will decrease to the point that it attracts larger investors and achieves widespread adoption. The bottom line is cryptocurrencies will remain volatile over the short-term, but they will become widely adopted over the long-term. There's no doubt that cryptocurrencies promise to revolutionize our world while simultaneously creating massive decentralized economies without intermediaries.

I've been looking for the best cryptocurrency guides to learn more about digital currencies and have realized that useful information is seriously lacking. With so much buzz and clutter of information out there, it is difficult to find the right guide.

This book explains everything you need to know about cryptocurrencies. It contains simple walkthroughs and interesting discussions to ensure that you really understand the basics of crypto. After you've read it, you'll be satisfied knowing that you learned more about the topic and can apply your knowledge to your investments.

I can't promise you that it will be easy to make money off of crypto, because, to be honest, many times it won't be. If you're willing to put in the time and effort, I promise this guide will give you the tools you need to become wealthy by investing in cryptocurrencies.

Thank you for purchasing this book. If you enjoyed reading this book, please leave a review or recommend it to others so they may benefit from it too.

Table of Contents

Chapter 1

What is Bitcoin

B itcoin is a new form of digital currency – a digital kind of cash, such as the US dollar or Euro. The concept behind Bitcoin is a decentralized, peer to peer network for digital payments. Bitcoin does not have to go through a bank or any intermediary, due to its decentralized architecture.

Bitcoin is also a distributed ledger, meaning that it records every transaction and every Bitcoin wallet's balance. Invented in 2008 with a publication titled "Bitcoin: A Peer-to-Peer Electronic Cash System," Bitcoin is a digital currency that combines earlier developments in digital currencies with the concept of decentralization. Bitcoin does not rely on any intermediary for transaction validation or currency issuance.

Bitcoin relies on its unique distributed ledger, the blockchain, for storing transactions, rather than being stored with banks. Users can interact with the blockchain through wallet software. For security, each wallet has its own private and public key – the public key being the Bitcoin address used to allow anyone to send you bitcoins, and the private key being the key that the owner uses to gain access to his wallet.

History of Cryptocurrency

The history of cryptography-based currencies dates back to 1983 when David Chaum introduced the idea of digital cash. In 1990, David Chaum founded DigiCash, an electronic cash solution in Amsterdam to commercialize the concept of digital currency, outside of the traditional financial system. The DigiCash transactions were also anonymous, like Bitcoin, as a result of cryptographic protocols (public and private keys) used in the currency.

However, it differed from Bitcoin as it was not decentralized. The synchronization of transactions happened on the company's central servers. The company failed to receive support and eventually filed for bankruptcy in 1998.

In 1998, a cryptocurrency called B-Money was slated to be introduced, focusing on anonymity and distributed methods of issuing coins. Similar to Bitcoin, the whitepaper suggested that digital pseudonyms could send and receive currency on a decentralized network. Unfortunately, B-Money never got off the ground.

Shortly after B-Money's whitepaper, Nick Szabo launched a similar project called Bit Gold. Bit Gold used a Proof-of-Work consensus model, similar to many consensus protocols used in mining today. Bit Gold moved away from centralized authorities as well. Satoshi Nakamoto also credits Nick Szabo's whitepaper as a precursor to the design of Bitcoin.

In 1997, a currency called HashCash was designed for a different purpose – limiting email spam. It used a Proof-of-Work algorithm for the generation and distribution of new coins, which also ended up being used in the Bitcoin protocol developed by Satoshi Nakamoto.

E-gold was the next digital currency to emerge, backed by gold held in a bank's safe deposit box. E-gold gained widespread adoption, with close to a million accounts by 2004. However, an increasing criminal usage of the currency led to its demise in 2005.

Further, it was at the same time that PayPal emerged in the US as an online payment system. In 2002, PayPal had its initial public offering and shortly after that, was acquired by eBay for USD 1.5 billion. PayPal continues to be one of the most popular payment systems on the Internet today.

Proof-of-Work

A key innovation that Bitcoin uses is a distributed computation system, called a 'Proof-of-Work' algorithm, allowing the decentralized network to arrive at a consensus about the state of transactions every 10 minutes. The system solves the double-spend problem, where a single currency unit could be spent twice. Previously, the problem of double-spending was cited as a weakness of digital currencies and could only be addressed by processing all transactions through a central clearing-house.

Since there is no central server, bitcoins are created through a process called 'mining,' which involves looking for a solution to a difficult mathematical problem. Any participant in the Bitcoin network that is running a full Bitcoin client wallet may operate as a miner, using their computer's processing power to try and find the 'nonce,' the solution to the Proof-of-Work mining algorithm round.

The difficulty of the algorithm that miners solve is adjusted dynamically so that, on average, miners find a correct answer every 10 minutes, regardless of how many miners are working on the problem at any instance. This innovation is a critical component that underpins Bitcoin's security and value.

Uses of Bitcoin

Bitcoin is designed to do anything that can be done with conventional currencies, such as buying and selling goods, sending money to people and organizations, or extending credit. However, unlike traditional currencies, Bitcoin is entirely virtual. There are no physical bitcoins in circulation.

The Bitcoin network includes features of encryption and digital signatures to ensure the security of the Bitcoin network. Bitcoins can be purchased, sold and exchanged for other currencies at specialized cryptocurrency exchanges.

Value of Bitcoin

The value of Bitcoin has often been questioned and has invited the ire of many people in the traditional finance world. Bitcoin's proponents argue that its value comes from the mining process and is derived from what people think it is worth, just like any other asset. Bitcoin's value is further solidified by its code and utility. A decentralized network of value exchange affords users substantial benefits, not previously available. If Bitcoin stops being useful, it will lose its value.

The utility of Bitcoin is the foundation of its value. However, the price speculation of Bitcoin over the last couple of years has mostly been fueled by investor interest as a store of value, similar to gold. Regardless of why participants choose to interact with the Bitcoin network, its value has started a broader conversation about the notion of analyzing value itself.

The Hard Cap on the Number of Bitcoin

Bitcoin limits the number of coins that can ever be created. There will only be 21 million bitcoins in existence. New bitcoins are created when miners solve a new block and are rewarded for their work, with new bitcoins and a portion of the transaction fees collected from the transactions in that specific block.

Every four years, the number of bitcoins created per block will be reduced by half, until 21 million bitcoins are eventually created. This is what gives Bitcoin its deflationary nature. Eventually, miners will only receive block rewards in the form of the collected transaction fees, and no more bitcoins will be created.

Withdrawal of the Inventor

In April 2011, Satoshi Nakamoto withdrew from the public, leaving the responsibility of developing the code and network to a growing group of volunteers. The name Satoshi Nakamoto is a pseudonym, and the identity of the person(s) behind Bitcoin is unknown.

Despite numerous people claiming to be the original Satoshi, none have been able to prove it. Further, there have been several mistaken identities, most notably a Japanese computer programmer named Satoshi Nakamoto that lived in California who was identified by the media. The same man eventually went on to refute the association with Bitcoin and is widely considered not to be him today.

Chapter 2

What is Blockchain Technology?

The blockchain is a timestamped, distributed public ledger accessible by everyone in the network, that updates close to real-time. The blockchain tracks each account on the Bitcoin network, known as a wallet. Every time a transaction is sent to the network, the sender digitally signs it and the transaction is propagated across the network, included in an upcoming block. A block is a group of transactions that get processed together and are mined by a miner in the network. Finally, the block is confirmed by the nodes in the network and the process restarts.

The blockchain, or the ledger of transactions, is a vertical stack of these blocks with the first block (also called the 'Genesis' block) serving as the foundation of all the other blocks. You can easily visualize the blockchain by imagining stacks of blocks on top of one another. The 'height' refers to the distance from the first block, and the 'top' refers to the most recently added block.

Each block within the blockchain has a 'hash' identifier, generated using a cryptographic algorithm. The hash of each block represents the entire state of the network up to that instance. Each block references a previous block, called the 'parent' block. Thus, each block contains the hash of its parent block as part of its own hash. This gives blockchains their permanent nature, as altering any prior block would change the most current block due to the hash value changing.

The sequence of blocks linking each other creates a chain going back all the way to the first block, which is called the blockchain.

Blockchain Is Immutable

Since every group of transactions (blocks) references the previous group, changing something would require altering the transaction history of all blocks in between the modified block and the current block, thereby invalidating the chain. Therefore, if someone wanted to go back and erase or replace an older transaction, they would invalidate the chain. The invalidation would require redoing the mathematical computations (Proof-of-Work) that make up the ledger until that point – which is practically impossible. Thus, the blockchain is immutable in nature.

When a transaction is sent to the network, it is recorded on the blockchain forever. Thus, no one has to depend on the word of either transacting party, as once the transaction is recorded on the blockchain, it is cryptographically verifiable, and there is no room for debate.

Blockchain Allows Anonymity

The blockchain uses cryptography to record, track and verify transactions. Participants can remain reasonably anonymous in their transactions, combining security with privacy. However, Bitcoin is not entirely anonymous; rather it is 'pseudonymous,' implying that the identifier does not give up their real-life identity but instead a Bitcoin address, quite like a pen-name of an author.

The Bitcoin public addresses are randomly generated alphanumerical sequences derived from the user's private key. It is difficult to track users and their transactions, but skilled analysis by experts has proven that it is possible to establish links between identity and Bitcoin addresses.

However, the debate persists on whether Bitcoin is anonymous or traceable, and the answer is both – everything is tracked on the blockchain, but users can keep their real-life identity hidden. Obfuscating your identity is primarily achieved by changing your public address for each transaction. Users can achieve a deeper level of anonymity by making sure to not associate their public address with purchases that could be linked to them or major cryptocurrency exchanges.

Blockchain Is Programmable

The blockchain is programmable, which give it numerous utilities that are still developing. For simplicity, a transaction that involves 'A sending B 1.5 BTC' could also be programmed to have certain conditions, such as 'A sends B 1.5 BTC, but B can only spend the 1.5 BTC after X days. Alternatively, B can only spend this BTC, when A signs off on it.'

Transaction Lifecycle

Each transaction is a public entry in Bitcoin's ledger, the blockchain. Once a transaction is recorded on the blockchain and confirmed by sufficient subsequent blocks, the transaction becomes a permanent part of the Bitcoin ledger and is accepted as valid by all participants.

The funds allocated to the new owner through the transaction can then be spent by him on other occasions, thereby extending the chain of ownership and beginning the lifecycle of a transaction again. In Bitcoin, all transactions are linked to each other in what is known as the Unspent Transaction Output Model (UTXO), and is the digital signature transaction scheme used in the network.

A transaction starts with its creation in the 'Coinbase' transaction, which is what the mining reward in BTC for miners is called. Subsequently followed by the authorization to spend the funds and send them to another network participant. The transaction is then broadcast on the Bitcoin network, where each network node validates and propagates the transaction until it reaches every node in the network. Finally, the transaction is recorded on the blockchain.

A transaction is an instrument that expresses the intent to transfer money, similar to a cheque facility in traditional banking.

Chapter 3

Buying Bitcoin

B itcoin is available for purchase through numerous avenues. The most common way is with a bank account, cash or PayPal.

Buying Bitcoin With A Bank Account

The purchasing of Bitcoin with a bank account is one of the quickest and easiest ways of obtaining Bitcoin anywhere in the world. Most of the services follow KYC (Know Your Customer) and AML (Anti-Money Laundering) laws, which one must comply with by providing information about their identity.

Many specialized exchanges allow buying Bitcoin using a bank account. There two most common web-based currency markets are:

Bitstamp (bitstamp.net), a European currency market that supports several currencies including Euros (EUR) and the US Dollar (USD).

Coinbase (coinbase.com), a US-based Bitcoin wallet and platform for transacting in Bitcoin and several other well-known cryptocurrencies.

The specific cryptocurrency exchange that you select will probably depend on the laws regarding cryptocurrencies in your country. Similar to opening a bank account, the services take several days or weeks to set up, and can even take months when there is a backlog of requests. Once you have an account set up on an exchange, you can buy and sell Bitcoin and other cryptos by depositing money into the exchange through bank wire or by using a linked debit card.

The following steps demonstrate how to buy Bitcoin on Coinbase:

Step #1: Open Coinbase

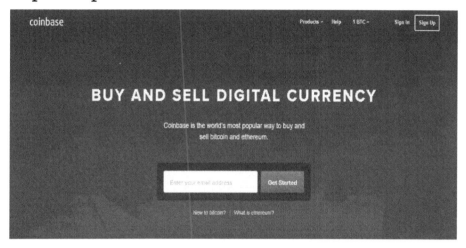

Step #2: Sign up on Coinbase

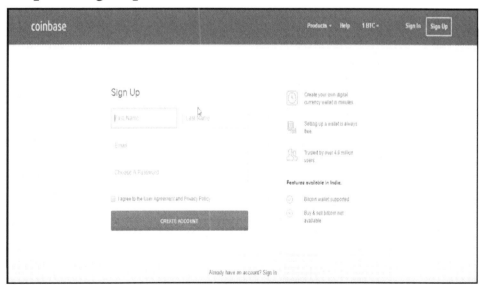

Step #3: Get email and mobile verified

Step #4: Add a payment method

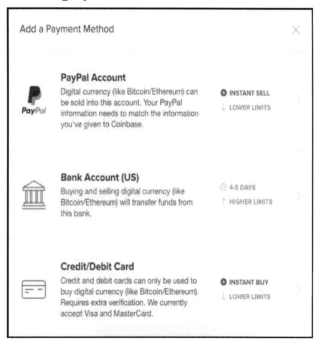

Step #5: Buying Bitcoin

The above image shows how to buy Bitcoin. Once the individual presses the 'Buy' option, the screen displays the currencies available to purchase, followed by the selection options for the payment method, and then asks for the amount that a user wishes to purchase.

Let's assume that we want to purchase $100 worth of Bitcoin. We input $100 in the amount of USD, and the exchange calculates the amount of bitcoin that we will receive for that USD amount. If Coinbase charges 1% fee for the transaction, it would translate to $1, which gets added to $100. The final amount we pay is $101.

Understanding How Fractions Work in Bitcoin

As you are purchasing Bitcoin, it is essential to understand that Bitcoin is a divisible currency and you do not need to buy one complete Bitcoin, but can engage in buying fractions of a Bitcoin.

To understand this, let's look at the divisibility of a dollar bill. Like a dollar bill can be divided into 100 cents, a Bitcoin is much more divisible and can be broken down to a hundred million equivalent small units, or the smallest unit called a 'Satoshi'. The breakdown is as follows:

1 Bitcoin = 100,000,000 Satoshi

0.1 Bitcoin = 10,000,000 Satoshi

0.01 Bitcoin = 1,000,000 Satoshi

Due to this, fractions of Bitcoin can be purchased and exchanged across the network. Eventually, this will allow for micro-payments and machine-to-machine payment networks.

Now, let's assume that currently, 1 Bitcoin equals $10,000. However, I have just decided to buy Bitcoin for a $100. So, I would receive a fraction of a Bitcoin, which can is calculated by:

$10,000 = 1 Bitcoin

Therefore, $100 = 1*(100/10,000) Bitcoin = 0.01 Bitcoin

For example, assume that there are no exchange fees (transaction costs). Now I own 0.01 Bitcoin, but one of my friends tells me that Bitcoin is the currency of the future and I should purchase more of it. So I decide to buy Bitcoin worth another $1,000.

$10,000 = 1 Bitcoin

Therefore, $1,000 = 1*(1,000/10,000) Bitcoin = 0.1 Bitcoin

Step #6: Confirmation

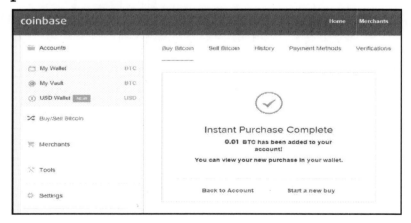

Safety In Entering Bank Details and Personal Information in Exchanges

As cryptocurrency exchanges require bank details and other personal information from an individual to conduct KYL/AML processes, users may be wary of sharing those details. Thus, it is important to understand how these exchanges protect user information before you submit your personal information to them.

The Safety Procedures Employed By Reputable Exchanges

Safety of sensitive information - Many of the most popular exchanges use bank-level encryption technologies to protect consumer data. For instance, Coinbase uses AES-256 encryption to store account details and routing numbers.

Employee checks and restricted access - The exchanges also conduct background checks on individuals before they are employed. Additionally, employee access to sensitive information is highly restricted, and many exchanges make use of trusted third-party intermediaries to facilitate account verification of users.

Two-factor authentication - The login to exchange websites usually requires two-factor authentication, meaning that no unauthorized login can happen on your account. The exchanges make use of either the Google Authenticator app or a mix of email and mobile authentication for each successful login attempt.

Follows respective jurisdictional laws - The reliable exchanges follow their jurisdiction's rules and regulations pertaining to online transactions.

No unjustifiable deductions - The exchanges also mention up-front that certain deductions, regarding transaction fees, shall be deducted. However, no other deductions are made by the exchanges.

Query/grievance redressal - The exchanges also have customer support in place for any grievances. Some may have a chat option, while others might respond to your query in using official mail.

It is essential to thoroughly check that the exchange an individual is making use of takes into consideration all the above security aspects.

Alternative sign-in - Signing up using an app

The process of signing up and buying Bitcoin can also be performed on the Coinbase app. The following graphics show the basic look and feel of the Coinbase app

Step #1: Download Coinbase app

Step #2: Sign up on Coinbase

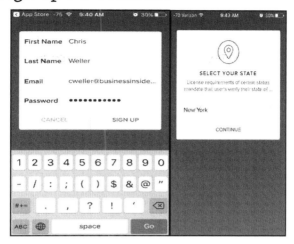

Step #3: Get email and mobile verified on the app

Step #4: Add payment method

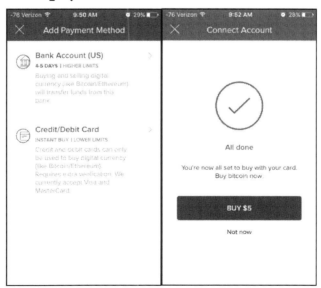

Chapter 4

Selling Bitcoin

When selling Bitcoin, there are several options available based on the customer's situation. There are two common ways to go about selling Bitcoin online:

1. Selling through an online exchange
2. Direct trade with another person

Selling through an online exchange

The exchanges act as an intermediary by holding funds and allowing the buying and selling of cryptocurrencies. A user can place a 'sell' order just like setting a buy order, stating the volume and type of currency they wish to sell, and the price they want to sell it.

As soon as someone places a matching buy order, the exchange automatically executes the order and updates both accounts. Many centralized cryptocurrency exchanges offer high volume trading, 24 hours a day. Further, they offer a suite of tools for day traders and other investors similar to mainstream tools used in traditional financial markets.

Taking the previous example where we first bought bitcoin worth $100 and then later worth $1,000, let us assume that it has been some time since the purchase. Now the price per bitcoin has gone up to $12,000.

Remember the individual that decided to sell Bitcoin that they purchased for $100 (it was 0.01 Bitcoin). Let's see how much he will be able to cash out that initial $100 purchase when the price of Bitcoin increases to $12,000.

1 Bitcoin = $12,000

0.01 Bitcoin = $12,000*0.01 = $120

The $100 was able to yield $120 over the course of the investment, a return of 20%.

To understand the selling process, let's use the Coinbase website once again. This time we will go to the 'sell' page and can view how our investments stack up against one another. The Coinbase website shows an equivalent USD amount next to our holdings in Bitcoin (BTC). Also, we can view any other cryptocurrencies that we hold on the exchange in the same view.

On the sell page, we will have the option to insert a sell amount as USD or as Bitcoin. Since we have decided to sell the 0.01 BTC that we bought earlier, we would write the amount '0.01' in the BTC box, and an equivalent amount in USD will automatically calculate.

The process for sell is demonstrated as follows:

Step #1: Open the sell page

Step #2: Place the sell order

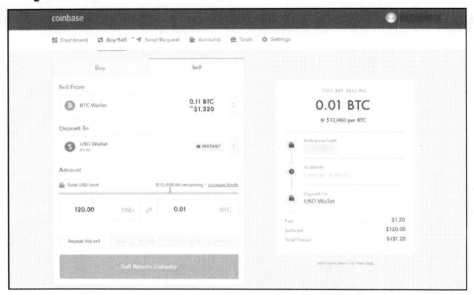

Chapter 5

How Can Bitcoin Change the Future?

Bitcoin and blockchain technology have the potential to change the status quo of the current financial paradigm. For the first time, people have an alternate option to fractional-reserve banking and the traditional investing model.

Bitcoin and other cryptocurrencies have the potential to disrupt numerous industries. Due to the significant reduction in the roles that intermediaries play, the opportunity for novel decentralized economies is just on the horizon.

Bitcoin For Remittance

Bitcoin is perfectly designed for remittances, sending money from one person to another, usually overseas. The remittances industry is enormous and is particularly important for individuals who live abroad and need to send money back to their families in their home countries.

Bitcoin allows users to cut out the middleman. Therefore, Bitcoin allows users to send value to another person on the other side of the world at a low cost. According to the World Bank, international remittances stood at US $700 billion in 2016, with banks and money transfer agencies taking 4% to 10% on the transferred amounts.

Bitcoin allows low-cost transactions beyond geographical boundaries, such as a 1% charge if using Bitcoin service providers like Coinbase. That should result in a minimum 3% savings on transactional costs, leaving more money for the recipient.

Direct Bitcoin payments between individuals typically only cost a few cents, no matter how large the transaction is. Since the Bitcoin blockchain ledger is transparent, users can see the amounts transacted across the network in real-time. Many of these transactions between users in different countries are for millions of dollars, for only a few cents.

Those who want to transfer any amount – small, medium or large – have a lot to gain from using Bitcoin. There are two primary roadblocks in the way of Bitcoin becoming a significant player in the remittance market:

1. Customer knowledge
2. Infrastructure.

Additionally, compared to traditional money remittance service, such as Western Union, where a receiver has to go to the Western Union office directly to pick up the money, Bitcoin does not require any physical office. Just as there is no difficulty in sending an email from a Gmail account to a Microsoft Outlook account, Bitcoin can be transmitted between individuals in the network, seamlessly.

Bitcoin For Micro-Transactions

Micro-transactions, or transactions ranging from a few cents to about five dollars, can be performed using Bitcoin. As Bitcoin is highly divisible, payments that require shelling out tiny amounts can be conducted just as effectively as using more substantial amounts.

Micro-transactions have tremendous potential, especially in the online economy. The traditional economy requires a lot of other costs besides the cost of a product. However, for electronic products, such as a computer game or a song, online micro-payments can play a major role in facilitating faster and more secure transactions.

Additionally, there is also the tipping economy, often used to show appreciation for services rendered. Social networks such as Reddit and Facebook have people tipping each other as a reward for posts they enjoy. Micro-payments help to make this process much more intuitive for all users, while not needing to integrate a third-party payment system into the social media network.

A more prominent form of tipping is the online donation market. Several popular podcasts and YouTube channels accept donations, which also are a significant source of their revenue. With Bitcoin, content creators can simply place Bitcoin addresses anywhere on the site and receive donations from a dedicated fan base. QR codes are especially useful in this scenario, and it is an online barcode that can be scanned by a user's Bitcoin wallet on their phone, and the payment information is automatically filled in.

Bitcoin For Crowdfunding

One of the most exciting developments in Bitcoin has been crowdfunding. The early known examples of crowdfunding include Kickstarter, which has been responsible for several influential innovations including virtual reality player Oculus, smart-watch Pebble, and many others. Cryptocurrencies can help secure crowdfunding in a more direct method, as asset tokens distributed on the blockchain.

The asset tokens represent ownership in the project, similar to shares in the company, which can be bought and sold on the blockchain. The blockchain represents a major opportunity for business owners to raise capital quickly.

The critical platform that allows for the issuance of tokens is Ethereum; however, there are many others such as Nxt, Neo and Cardano.

Banking for The Unbanked

According to a Bloomberg report, more than half of the World's population does not have a bank account. However, close to 75% of the population has mobile penetration. Therefore, Bitcoin payments using mobile devices/apps could enable financial transactions over far distances and at no extra cost.

New World Enterprises

A cryptocurrency platform is similar to a company. It offers financial services, miners represent optional employees, and those who hold the cryptocurrency are its shareholders. The company does not have any directors —as the blockchain can be pre-programmed with a specific set of business operations to run and operate the business.

The more forward-looking cryptocurrency platforms are focusing on decentralized governance, in the form of Decentralized Autonomous Organizations (DAOs). DAOs function as autonomous and self-executing organizations on the Internet whose direction is controlled directly by the holders of its native token.

Convenience in Moving Wealth

Someone can trivially transfer his or her assets to people in other countries using Bitcoin. However, let's assume someone holds wealth in the form of 10 gold bars that he or she would like to take along to the other country. The person may not be to able to achieve such a feat with ease, as there are risks of getting robbed, or meeting some police or government official at the border.

Moving your wealth with Bitcoin is near instantaneous, and is as simple as pressing a couple of buttons on your phone. Assets can even be tokenized and placed on the blockchain such as with Ethereum and similar platforms like Neo.

Bitcoin also is also fungible, where similar to the US Dollar, each Bitcoin is equal to the next Bitcoin. This means that all Bitcoin is worth the same. Further, Bitcoin cannot be counterfeited as the money supply and integrity of each Bitcoin is maintained through the UTXO model.

Responsible and Transparent Economy

Transparency in transactions can be brought about by Bitcoin, as the blockchain can be used for a land registry, asset ownership and ownership of precious assets. Since the blockchain is immutable, the owner-ship of assets is transparent for government records and financial audit-ing.

Additionally, the government can also keep check of the budget of its departments by using the blockchain to act as the ledger for the de-partment's operations. The result is increased efficiency and accounta-bility of department funding. The accounting for the budget would also significantly reduce the need for accountants and third-party audits.

Chapter 6

Do Stores Accept Bitcoin?

Since Bitcoin came into being, cryptocurrency enthusiasts have imagined a world where digital currencies can be used to make payments just like any other means of payment. While the likes of Amazon, JC Penny, and other major retailers do not accept Bitcoin (yet), there are a few online retailers that do accept payments in Bitcoin.

Overstock.com

In January 2014, Overstock became the first major online retailer to start accepting payments in Bitcoin. The company allowed its users to pay for items including laptops, television sets, pillows and other home furnishings to be purchased in Bitcoin.

Additionally, the online retailer also accepts other well-known cryptocurrencies such as Ethereum, Litecoin, Monero, Dash and Bitcoin Cash.

Expedia

In June 2014, Expedia, a massive online travel booking agency, began allowing users to pay for their hotel bookings with Bitcoin. Expedia teamed up with Coinbase to implement the new payment option.

However, despite Bitcoin payments currently limited to hotel bookings, they may be extended to flight payments soon.

Shopify

In November 2013, the e-commerce platform Shopify allowed its 75,000+ merchants the option to accept Bitcoin payments on their online shops set up using Shopify website. The company partnered with BitPay to receive Bitcoin payments.

Newegg

In July 2014, online electronics store Newegg allowed the use of Bitcoin to pay for computer hardware and software on its website. The company uses BitPay as the payment processor to convert Bitcoins sales into US dollars.

Lush

In July 2017, UK based cosmetics player Lush began accepting Bitcoin for cosmetic goods purchases on its website. The company intends to serve global customers and partner with global suppliers by allowing the use of Bitcoin.

Reeds Jewelers

Reeds Jewelers, an American brick-and-mortar jewelry store with a national online presence, accepts Bitcoin for the purchase of jewelry, including watches and loose diamonds.

Pizza for Coins

The site allows paying for pizza at famous joints (Dominos, Pizza Hut or Papa John's) using the digital currency. However, a fee is added to the total billed amount.

Several other companies have also begun accepting Bitcoin.

Virgin Galactic

In November 2013, UK-based spacecraft company Virgin Galactic also announced their acceptance of Bitcoin payments as a way to pay for future journeys into space.

Zynga

In the same month, social gaming company Zynga announced they too were accepting Bitcoin as an in-app payment option in select games, also enabled by the payment processor BitPay.

eGifter

In April 2014, gift card site eGifter enabled the purchase of gift cards using Bitcoin. These gift cards can be used at several retailers including Amazon, JCPenny, Sephora, Home Depot and many more.

Wikipedia

The online community-based encyclopedia Wikipedia is currently accepting Bitcoin as donations. The Wikipedia Foundation partnered with Coinbase to process the donations, where Coinbase offered to waive processing fees for the non-profit organization.

DISH Network

In August 2014, satellite TV and internet service provider DISH Network began accepting Bitcoin payments by partnering with Coinbase to enable such transactions.

PayPal

In April 2015, PayPal announced that merchants could start accepting payments using Bitcoin. The company partnered with Braintree, Coinbase, BitPay and GoCoin to enable the Bitcoin integration in its merchant payments platform (PayPal Payments Hub).

Steam

In April 2016, gaming platform Steam allowed the buying of games using Bitcoin. The parent company of the Steam platform, Valve, partnered with BitPay to enable Bitcoin payments.

Microsoft

Microsoft allows using Bitcoin to purchase games, movies, and apps in the Windows and Xbox stores.

Chapter 7

The Dangers of Cryptocurrency

Ever since cryptocurrencies have gained popularity, regulators have warned investors about the dangers surrounding the market. Some of the hazards of cryptocurrency investing are as follows:

Market Manipulation

Since Bitcoin is limited in nature (limited to 21 million that can ever be created, with close to 16.7 million in circulation), there is the possibility of it being concentrated in the hands of a few, which can lead to high market manipulation. Therefore, investment in Bitcoin is highly speculative, as a few whales with can change market dynamics quickly.

Security Concerns

The holders of crypto, whether they are trading platforms, exchanges, or retail investors, are a lucrative target for hackers. There have been incidents in the past where exchanges have been hacked and Bitcoin stolen. The losses are unrecoverable when Bitcoin is taken from these exchanges and virtual wallets.

Unregulated and Not Backed By an Asset

The market is largely unregulated, with no option of legal recourse in case of any conflict in a transaction. Therefore, one must carefully investigate the seller before purchasing Bitcoin. Additionally, Bitcoin and other virtual currencies are not fiat currencies, as they are not backed by the United States or any other government or central bank.

High Volatility

The value of Bitcoin fluctuates regularly and can vary significantly in a concise period; therefore, you must prepare for radical changes in the value of your Bitcoin investment, including sizeable single day drops or increases in the value. Some argue that good currencies have low volatility, as owning a highly volatile currency or accepting it as a form of payment is too risky.

Experimental Currency

Bitcoin is based on a public ledger called the "Blockchain," which is still experimental in nature and could be subject to changes, errors, or criminal activity that could adversely affect Bitcoin's value.

Government Regulations

If the government decides to declare owning Bitcoin illegal, there might be significant panic in the market. Currently, the government's stance on cryptocurrencies is not clear, and the danger is as real as Bitcoin. It is somewhat of a competitor to government-issued currency.

Competition

Other cryptocurrencies could make Bitcoin a thing of the past. Several cryptocurrencies offer faster transactions, complete anonymity, storage space and other improvements which could lead to lower market share for Bitcoin.

No Safety Mechanisms

Bitcoin can be accessed by an individual using his private key or secret phrase which protect his wallet. However, if you lose your key and secret phrase, the funds will be lost forever. Since there's no support, method to recover the password, and no way to verify your identity, when it's gone - it's gone for good.

Quantum Computers

As computers become more advanced, especially with the emergence of Quantum computers, powerful computers may be able to break

Bitcoin's security through brute forcing its hashing algorithm. A crucial feature of Bitcoin is its security; however, Quantum computers can potentially solve the basic security components of Bitcoin in the future. With the first Quantum computers currently under development, the danger posed by quantum computers is still a few years away, but worth watching.

Ponzi Schemes

As there is a great deal of misinformation among the ordinary people regarding Bitcoin trading, fraudsters can take advantage of this by launching Ponzi schemes, such as schemes guaranteeing "immediate high returns."

Chapter 8

Can Bitcoin Be Hacked?

Bitcoin, the decentralized digital currency, is almost impossible to hack as each block that forms the basis of the blockchain needs a consensus before it can permanently join the blockchain. Bitcoin is continuously under review by other Bitcoin users.

Bitcoin is no more at risk than other payment methods such as PayPal or traditional credit cards. In fact, it is actually at less risk. While the fact that Bitcoin cannot be hacked offers a major relief, the actual usage of Bitcoin is full of vulnerabilities.

Take Precautions In Transactions

It is essential to take precautions that minimize the risk of being hacked.

First, the exchanges that offer Bitcoin are vulnerable if specific precautions are not taken. Hackers can use snooping tools or phishing attacks to find passwords. Therefore, it is always advisable to use two-factor authentications (2FA) at Bitcoin exchanges. Two-Factor authentication allows a notification to be sent to the linked cell phone to validate a login or a transaction.

Second, users should not keep their digital currency holdings on an exchange. However, they should practice maintaining the bulk of their Bitcoin in a 'cold wallet,' an offline wallet not connected to the Internet.

Third, users should not speak publicly about their cryptocurrency wallets, especially on platforms like Facebook and Telegram. Further, users should be on the lookout for suspicious activity, especially notifications of s SIM swap or port.

Fourth, users should set a long and hard password, and should not share access to the password with others.

The guidelines for minimizing the risk of being targeted by a hacker are quite similar to the risk mitigation efforts needed in banking transactions.

Recognize Scams

There is a second kind of scam that is tough to recognize, a Ponzi scheme. Several companies will offer a service, called 'cloud mining.' They will mine for users while users 'rent' the hardware from them.

Could mining is just a front, while actually, the mining profits are coming from the proceeds of new investors – a Ponzi scheme.

As cloud mining becomes less popular, primarily due to the number of scams reported, there will be new scams in place. Such scams include individual or company paying out day trading profits on your proceeds.

Remain cautious about getting into such activities. Also, the mining is easily verifiable on the blockchain, and therefore, if the service cannot present an address with the creation of new coins through mining, it should not be trusted at all.

As with every other business, there will be people trying to take advantage of gullible investors. Another measure to probe companies is getting onto popular social media outlets (such as Reddit, Quora, Facebook) and looking for customer reviews.

Chapter 9

What Do I Need To Get Going?

There are several terms that you will come across in the world of Bitcoin. These can range from the mining of Bitcoin to holding bitcoins (HODL) or other cryptocurrencies.

Mining-Related Terminologies

Mining

Mining is the process that confirms Bitcoin transactions. The participants in the network solve increasingly difficult mathematical equations to find 'blocks' on the blockchain, which happens roughly every 10 minutes.

Mining is an integral part of cryptocurrencies that use Proof-of-Work, as it involves adding transaction records to the public ledger. It's the process that reaches a consensus, the critical component of making the decentralized system work.

Miner

A miner is someone who is involved in the process of mining Bitcoin. During the mining process, the miners receive rewards – usually a certain number of cryptocurrency coins. Anyone can be a miner – they just need to have an Internet connection and correct hardware.

Block

A block is a group of transactions chained to the previous block on the blockchain. Every block contains a condensed version of the last block – therefore, it is not possible to change a previous transaction.

Transaction Reward

The miners are rewarded a small number of Bitcoin every time they correctly solve a block, through a combination of transaction fees and new bitcoins created (until the 21 millio limit is reached).

Hashing Power

The total computing power determines the complexity of mathematical equations, called the hashing power, on the network.

Difficulty of Mining

The difficulty of mining is adjusted every 2,016 blocks based on how quickly the last 2,016 blocks were solved.

Application-Specific Integration Circuit (ASIC)

The mining of Bitcoin grew from CPU to GPU (graphics processing unit) that are meant for gaming-focused computers. Once that power became widespread in the market, the majority of mining switched to ASICs which are specific chips created for efficient mining. ASICs dominate the mining market today.

Full Node

Running a full node means downloading the entire Bitcoin blockchain which helps double-checking transactions already confirmed by miners. While it does not reap any rewards, it contributes to the Bitcoin network in a charitable way. There have been discussions about adding a reward incentive for running a full node.

Mining Pool

Most of the mining is done in pools. Pool mining is when a group of miners decides to group their hashing power and share the rewards. The approach depends on trust since the individual miners have to trust the pool operator to give out the rewards appropriately.

Cloud Mining

Cloud mining is a scheme wherein mining companies build giant warehouse-sized mining farms, sell or lease little pieces of those farms to customers, and after taking their fee, pay customers based on the proportion of hashing percentage they own.

Pre-Mining

Pre-mining is when developers allocate a specific quantity of credit to a particular crypto-address before actually releasing the source code to the open network. The creators get to keep part of the token to themselves. Thus, it mainly refers to all coins that have been mined before being officially launched.

Pre-mining comes with negative connotations, as the developers are deemed to be taking unfair advantage by allocating funds before the official launch or simply by self-mining before releasing the information about the coin to other miners.

Since there are no other miners yet involved in the mining process, the difficulty of the computational math remains relatively low, meaning they can mine much quicker. By the time the coins are made public, the team already has a significant proportion of the coins.

Instamine

Instamine refers to coins being distributed during the first few blocks when the difficulty of mining is low. At this time, mining can be performed almost instantly, hence the name Instamine.

Bitcoin is also an example of Instamine, as the creator of Bitcoin – Satoshi Nakamoto, has a high percentage of the total amount of Bitcoins available.

Faucet

Several websites and apps provide a reward system for giving out Satoshis (which is one-hundredth of a millionth of a unit of Bitcoin). These specific sites or apps are called Faucets. However, these faucets usually hold onto coins that are rewarded to visitors until the holdings have reached a certain threshold.

The purpose of giving out fractions of Bitcoin for free is part of a broader introduction to Bitcoin plan. In the beginning, faucets were developed to help spread the word of Bitcoin. Currently, these faucets are used for the same purpose but for altcoins.

It allows users to test these new coins before actually committing to buying them. It's an excellent way of promoting digital currency and bringing in new users.

Faucets can help websites get traffic. They are high-traffic sites, like any site that gives away free money can quickly retain large numbers of daily page views. Sites that have content related to Bitcoin or cryptocurrency can use a faucet to bring more people to the site and learn about the brand.

Trading Terminologies

HODL

When an individual enters into the world of Bitcoin with the intention of investing, there is one piece of advice that an enthusiast would give him in the domain, HODL. HODL is a humorous misspelling of 'hold' in the crypto community. As the day by day stability is relatively low in the cryptocurrencies due to their high volatility, the would-be investors are asked to buy and hold.

Bitcoin has seen several spikes in its history, which have shown a similar pattern in its price. First, the coin would drop in value slightly; then it would jump to unprecedented heights. Subsequently, it falls a substantial amount – to half its value or less, but always above the previous jump's value. Later, it jumps to heights that dwarf the last rise.

Pump and Dump

It is a trading term that increasingly used in cryptocurrencies. The basic idea of investing – buy when the price is low and sell when it is high, is often used by high profile investors to pump and dump the market.

A group of large users, known as the whales, promote or endorse a particular coin to artificially increase the price. These whales start by buying cheap coins and build up a hype surrounding the specific cryptocurrency.

Once the coin reaches a particular price, the 'dump' begins wherein the whales start selling their coins. This sends ripples of panic through the market, and people start panic-selling.

Shorting

The term 'shorting' is common in stock markets, where the investor bets that the price of the cryptocurrency will go down. Therefore, if the prices do go down, the investor will win money. In other words, it is possible to make money when the price of a cryptocurrency falls.

Volatility

Volatility refers to the risk and uncertainty about the changes in the value of a cryptocurrency. High volatility means that value is unpredictable and can dramatically change quickly. In traditional markets, it is considered a risky investment.

On the other hand, lower volatility means the value of the coin doesn't change that significantly; instead, it remains at a stable rate over a particular period.

Volatility can be a great way to understand the pricing behavior of a particular currency.

Whale

'Whale' is a common term in the cryptocurrency market used to describe big cryptocurrency account holders. They are compared to whales as they can overpower the smaller players in the market.

Initial coin Offering (ICO)

A popular way to launch a coin these days is through an Initial Coin Offering (ICO). The ICO is a way of crowdfunding a new cryptocurrency. It is a similar concept to an IPO (Initial Public Offering) as both the processes are where companies raise capital.

However, there is a crucial difference in the sense that ICO gives the investor returns in the form of a cryptocurrency, whereas an investor would receive securities in the case of an IPO. These cryptocurrencies are also known as tokens, specifically ERC-20 tokens on Ethereum.

Most ICOs distribute tokens providing investors access to the particular project, instead of ownership in the company. The ICOs are usually open for a few weeks to a couple of months. Unlike an IPO, which is a one-off event, an ICO can also take place multiple times.

Market Capitalization

Market capitalization is a method of ranking the size of a specific cryptocurrency and is calculated by multiplying the circulating supply by the price of the currency. Market cap is as a way of showing the relative size and risk of a specific cryptocurrency.

Cryptocurrency Consensus Terminologies

PoW – Proof-of-Work

PoW is a type of cryptocurrency that has algorithms that reward the participants who manage to solve a mathematical puzzle for validating transactions and creating new blocks on the chain.

PoS – Proof-of-Stake

Proof-of-Stake is another type of consensus mechanism in cryptocurrencies, which helps the cryptocurrency blockchain network achieve distributed consensus without the consumption of electricity. In POS-based cryptocurrencies, the odds of an account selected for mining of the block depends on its wealth, or in other words, its stake.

The blocks in POS cryptocurrencies are created or shaped, rather than mined. The creators of these are sometimes known as forgers.

Bots

As Bitcoin and altcoins are continually witnessing price changes, the trading bots help traders analyze charts and patterns in movement all day, all week. As a result, using trading bots provides a relief for those that don't have the time to manage their accounts, and let the trading bots do it for them.

Chapter 10

What is a Virtual Wallet?

A cryptocurrency wallet is a secure digital wallet used to store, send, and receive digital currency like Bitcoin. Most coins have an official wallet and a few officially recommended third-party wallets.

Similar to a traditional wallet carried in a pocket, a Bitcoin wallet is used to store money. The difference is that instead of storing a collection of bills and cards, a Bitcoin wallet stores a group of Bitcoin private keys. Typically, a wallet is encrypted with a password or otherwise protected from unauthorized access.

Working of Cryptocurrency Wallet

In the wallet, a private key (secure digital code known only to you and your wallet) stores ownership of a public key (a public digital code connected to a certain amount of currency). Thus, the wallet stores private and public keys, which allows for sending and receiving coins. It also shows a personal ledger of transactions to the user.

Security of Cryptocurrency Wallets

Cryptocurrency wallets are all built to be secure, but the exact protection differs from wallet to wallet. Generally, apart from usernames and passwords, the security of wallets come from two-factor authentication, such as using a mobile phone to authenticate login or transaction on the exchange.

Recently, Google Authenticator has been used for extra layers of protection, thereby encrypting one's wallet. Also, users can also use multi-signature transactions.

Types of Wallets

There are many different types of wallets you can use to hold your Bitcoin and other cryptocurrencies. These include online, offline, mobile, hardware, desktop, and paper wallets. Each type refers to the medium the portfolio is stored on.

Some wallets offer more than one method of accessing the wallet. For instance, Bitcoin Wallet is a desktop application and a mobile app.

Desktop Wallet

Desktop Wallets are one of the most common forms of wallets. They are hosted on a personal computer (desktop) rather than being stored on a company's servers.

However, the security of the wallet is highly dependent on the safety of the personal computer. Thus, if you decide to get a desktop wallet, it is vital to secure your computer with anti-virus protection and be cautious of any download from unknown sites.

Mobile Wallet

This is a wallet that operates on a smartphone or tablet as a kind of mobile app. While not as secure as full-client desktop wallets, some mobile wallets retain high-security features.

Further, if you plan to use cryptocurrency for purchases at any brick-and-mortar store, having the app on your phone is essential. Some mobile wallets have additional support for NFC (Near Field Communications) payments.

People can use these as a tap-and-pay kind of system, sending cryptocurrencies directly to the seller that accepts this kind of payment.

Online Wallet

The online wallet is a web-based wallet that is hosted on a real or virtual server, rather than on a downloaded app. The good thing about web-based wallets is that you can access them from any device.

However, it is also a disadvantage, as using a web-based wallet requires you to trust a third-party company to take care of your coins.

Hardware Wallet

Dedicated hardware wallets, such as USB devices, are specially built to hold cryptocurrencies and keep them secure. These devices can also be accessed online to make transactions and retrieve data, and can also be taken offline for transportation and security.

Paper Wallet

You can print out a QR code for both public and private keys, which allow you to both send and receive digital currencies using a paper wallet. This can allow you to avoid storing digital data about your money entirely.

Chapter 11

What are Exchanges?

Cryptocurrency exchanges are websites where you can buy, sell or exchange cryptocurrencies for other digital currencies or traditional currencies (like US dollars or Euro). There are several aspects that you need to consider before choosing an exchange.

Reputation

You must look at the reputation of exchanges by going through reviews from individual users as well as popular industry websites. Additionally, you can also ask questions on forums like BitcoinTalk or Reddit.

Fees

There are fees associated with trading on most exchanges. You should understand the deposit, transaction and withdrawal fees in the fee-related information page on their websites before joining. The fees can differ substantially depending on the exchange you use.

Payment Methods

Users should explore the payment methods available on the exchange. The payment methods available on a website may vary from credit and debit card, wire transfer, PayPal, among others.

Users must ensure that the available payment methods are suitable or it would inconvenience the user to operate on an exchange with limited payment options.

Proof of Identity

The purchase of cryptocurrencies will usually require identity verification. Further, payment by credit cards may come with a premium price as there is a higher risk of fraud, and higher transaction and processing fees.

In addition, the purchase of cryptocurrencies via wire transfer may take significantly longer as banks take time to process.

The vast majority of the Bitcoin trading platforms in the US and the UK require ID verification to make deposits & withdrawals. Verification may take a few days, and it protects the exchange against scams and money laundering.

In several geographical locations, the exchanges are mandated to have KYC (Know Your Customer) requirements by regulators.

Geographical Restrictions

Certain exchanges can limit specific user functions to only be accessible from individual countries. It makes sense to ensure that the exchange allows full access to all platform tools and features in the country you currently live in.

Exchange Rate

The exchange rate used by different exchanges may vary. The prices of purchasing Bitcoin will change as a result of varying exchange rates.

The Best Cryptocurrency Exchanges

To buy and sell Bitcoin and other cryptocurrencies, there are many exchanges to choose from, but not all exchanges offer the same kind of services. The experience on each exchange may range in criteria such as user reviews, user-friendliness, accessibility, fees, and security.

Coinbase

Coinbase is one of the most popular and well-known brokers and trading platforms in the world, backed by trusted investors and used by millions of customers globally.

The Coinbase platform makes it easy to buy, use, store and trade digital currency securely. The users can purchase Bitcoins, Ethereum and Litecoin from Coinbase through a digital wallet available on Android and iPhone. The trading with other users can happen with other users on the company's Global Digital Asset Exchange (GDAX) subsidiary.

GDAX does not currently charge any transfer fees for moving funds between your Coinbase account and GDAX account.

The exchange has an excellent reputation and is highly secure. The fees charged are reasonable and has a beginner friendly interface. Coinbase insurance also covers the stored currency.

However, the exchange has limited payment methods, limited country support and GDAX is suitable for technical traders only.

Kraken

Founded in 2011, Kraken is a large Bitcoin exchange in volume and liquidity. The exchange lets you buy and sell Bitcoin, and trade between bitcoins and Euros, US Dollars, Canadian Dollars, British Pounds and Japanese Yen.

It is also possible to trade digital currencies other than Bitcoin including Ethereum, Monero, Ethereum Classic, Augur REP tokens, ICONOMI, Zcash, Litecoin, Dogecoin, Ripple and Stellar/Lumens, among others.

Additionally, for the more experienced users, Kraken offers margin trading and a host of other trading features.

The exchange has a good reputation, decent exchange rates, and low transaction fees. The exchange also charges minimal deposit fees and has excellent user support. The best part about the exchange is that it is secure and supported worldwide.

However, the exchange has limited payment methods, and may not be suitable for beginners due to its unintuitive user interface.

Cex.io

Cex.io provides a wide range of services for using Bitcoin and other cryptocurrencies. The platform lets users easily trade fiat money for cryptocurrencies and vice versa.

For the professional traders, the platform offers personalized and user-friendly trading dashboards and margin trading.

The Cex.io website is secure, intuitive, and cryptocurrencies can be stored in safe cold storage.

The exchange has a solid reputation, a good mobile product and supports credit cards. Also, the exchange is beginner friendly, has a decent exchange rate and is supported worldwide.

However, the exchange has a lengthy verification process, and depositing is quite expensive, especially with the credit card.

ShapeShift

ShapeShift is one of the leading exchanges that supports a variety of cryptocurrencies including Bitcoin, Ethereum, Monero, Zcash, Dash, Dogecoin among others. It is an excellent exchange for those who want to make instant, straightforward trades without signing up to an account or relying on a platform to hold their funds.

However, ShapeShift does not allow users to purchase cryptos with debit cards, credit cards or any other payment system. The platform has a no fiat policy and only allows for the exchange between Bitcoin and the other supported cryptocurrencies.

The exchange has a great reputation and is beginner-friendly. The number of cryptos available for trade is vast, and the exchange provides reasonable prices.

Poloniex

Founded in 2014, Poloniex is one of the world's leading cryptocurrency exchanges. The exchange offers a secure trading environment with more than 100 different Bitcoin cryptocurrency pairs.

The exchange also offers advanced tools and data analysis for sophisticated traders. As one of the most popular trading platforms with the highest trading volumes, users will always be able to close a trade position.

The fees on the exchange may range from 0.10 to 0.25%. There are no fees for withdrawals beyond the transaction fee required by the network.

The exchange allows for expedited account creation, high-volume lending, user-friendly interface and low trading fees.

However, the exchange has a slow customer service and no fiat support.

Chapter 12

How to Encrypt Your Wallet

Bitcoin makes it possible to transfer value anywhere and allows you to be in control of your money. However, such features come with significant security concerns and the wallet must be secured just like a real-life wallet.

At the same time, Bitcoin can provide very high levels of security if used correctly. Therefore, it is imperative to adopt good practices to protect money.

Be Careful With Online Services

The services designed to store money online must be reviewed cautiously, as many exchanges and online wallets have suffered from security breaches in the past. Many services generally do not provide enough insurance and security to be used to store money like a bank.

Additionally, using two-factor authentication (2FA) is recommended.

Small Amounts For Everyday Uses

A Bitcoin wallet is similar to a physical wallet with cash. Just as you would not keep too much money in your pocket, you might consider the same for your Bitcoin wallet.

In general, it is a good practice to keep only small amounts of bitcoins for everyday use and keep the remaining part of your funds in a safer environment.

Backup Your Wallet

A backup wallet, stored in a safe place, can protect you against computer failures and human mistakes. It can also allow you to recover your wallet in case the mobile or computer is stolen or has gone defunct.

However, some wallets contain hidden private keys internally. If the backup is taken only from the visible Bitcoin addresses, you might not be able to recover a significant portion of your funds with the backup.

Encrypt Online Backups

A backup that is stored online is highly vulnerable to theft. Additionally, even a computer that is connected to the Internet is vulnerable to malicious software.

Thus, encrypting any backup that is exposed to the network is a good security practice.

Use Many Secure Locations

It is important to note that single points of failure can be dangerous for security and if the backup is not dependent on a single location, it is more secure. Be advised and take into consideration that using different media like USB's, paper wallet, and digital wallets are useful for distributing holdings.

Make Regular Backups

The backup of wallet should be done on a regular basis to ensure that all recent Bitcoin change addresses and new addresses created are included in the backup.

Encrypt Wallet

Encrypting the wallet on a smartphone allows you to set a password for any effort to withdraw funds. This helps you to protect against thieves.

Never Forget Your Password

You should never forget your password as the funds may get permanently lost. Unlike a bank, there are virtually no password recovery options with Bitcoin.

Your password should be one that is easy to remember even after many years without using it. This can be achieved by keeping a paper copy of the password in a safe place like a vault.

Using a Strong Password

A password that contains only letters or recognizable words can be considered weak and easy to break. Therefore, a strong password that contains letters, numbers and other special characters should be considered.

Offline Wallet for Savings

An offline wallet, also known as a cold storage wallet, provides the highest level of security for savings. It involves storing a wallet in a secure place that is not connected to the Internet.

Keep the Software Up to Date

It is always advisable to use the latest version of Bitcoin software to be able to receive all the critical stability and security fixes. The updates can prevent problems, as well as include new useful features and help keep the wallet safe.

Installing updates for all other software on your computer or mobile is also essential to keep your wallet environment safer.

Multi-Signature to Protect Against Theft

A multi-signature feature can allow a transaction to require multiple independent approvals to be spent.

This can be used by an organization to give its members access to its treasury while requiring a withdrawal to have multiple members sign the transaction.

Chapter 13

A Look at Some Altcoins

Ethereum

The same way that Bitcoin is popularized as a Satoshi Nakamoto's legacy, Ethereum has popularized another crypto-genius, called Vitalik Buterin.

Similar to Bitcoin, Ethereum runs on blockchain technology but with a different purpose. On the one hand, Bitcoin blockchain focuses on keeping track of ownership of the cryptocurrency via peer-to-peer electronic cash system. The primary purpose of Ethereum, on the other hand, is to run the programming code of a decentralized application.

Ethereum allows running small programs on the blockchain, called 'smart contracts.' These smart contracts help design an electronic commerce protocol that can automate the enforcement and execution of an agreement.

For instance, A trusts B, but A does not trust C, who will deliver A's packet to B. Thus, A wants to make a payment only when B says the goods have been delivered.

With smart contracts, A makes a payment for a shipment to a smart contract on a day of loading. It holds payment until shipment is delivered by C to B. Then the smart contract releases the payment, and the money is transferred to C automatically.

The Ages of Blockchain

Bitcoin is Blockchain 1.0

Bitcoin, the first digital cryptocurrency, was introduced as a novel idea to be used as a currency, where transactions are recorded on the blockchain. Blockchain allows transactions to be permanent in nature, meaning they cannot be altered.

Ethereum is Blockchain 2.0

Ethereum, the platform that enables smart contracts and decentralized application (dApps), allows applications to be built using blockchain technology.

It provides two uses:

1. A cryptocurrency
2. A platform to run applications. The smart contracts and dApps bring a new level of versatility to the currency as it can be used to build a large number of apps on top of it.

However, currently, there is much talk about a move by certain currencies towards blockchain 3.0

Specific Currencies Trying to Start the Blockchain 3.0 Era

Cardano and some other currencies are claiming to be blockchain 3.0 projects, in the sense that they intend to offer interoperability with other currencies and scalability for a large number of transactions.

Litecoin

It is known as "the silver to Bitcoin's gold" and is a digital currency that emerged after Bitcoin. The cryptocurrency is almost four times faster, with more tokens and a minimized algorithm.

It is considered a backup option for those who are aware of the problems with Bitcoin.

Just like Bitcoin, Litecoin is a cryptocurrency that is generated through Proof-of-Work mining. Litecoin was created in October 2011 by former Google engineer Charles Lee.

The key difference for end-users is the 2.5-minute time required to generate a block, as opposed to Bitcoin's 10 minutes. Charles Lee also works for Coinbase, one of the most popular online Bitcoin wallets and exchange.

Transaction Differences

The main difference is that Litecoin can confirm transactions must faster than Bitcoin. The implications of that are that a merchant who chooses to wait for a minimum of two confirmations would only need to wait five minutes in case of Litecoin, whereas they would have to wait 20 minutes for two confirmations with Bitcoin.

Monero

The Monero algorithm emerged with more security in mind than Bitcoin. It added additional privacy features to the chain.

In the case of Bitcoin, every transaction is documented and can be traced back to its origins; however, Monero focuses on anonymity. It introduced an algorithm called ring-signatures, which allows processing transactions, while completely obfuscating the amounts transacted, and sender/receiver identities. This makes it one of the most anonymous cryptocurrencies available on the market.

Introduction to Ring Signatures

Ring signatures are digital signatures which can be performed by any member of a ring or group, and it enables a transaction muddling effect, where the involved parties are hidden.

This means that when money is sent, it is sent as a group of randomly picked ring signed transactions. Thus, an incoming transaction is coming as a group of transactions each with the same chance of being the actual sender.

This makes Monero a top choice for maintaining both sender and receiver privacy.

Stealth Addresses

Monero also makes use of stealth addresses which take care of the recipient's privacy. The stealth addresses do not allow a third party to see any transactions completed.

When a transaction is done on the Monero blockchain, it doesn't list the public address of the receiver on the blockchain but instead creates a new one-time destination address which is not linked to a receiver's public address.

Obfuscation of IP using KOVARI

Kovari, an open-source technology that hides the IP addresses of users while transacting with Monero, uses both routing techniques and encryption to hide the IP addresses. Further, it masks the geographical location of transaction origins and destinations by creating a new layer over the Internet.

This is expected to make Monero the most trusted, open source, decentralized, and fully anonymous cryptocurrency.

Difference From Bitcoin

Monero is a cryptocurrency like Bitcoin, but unlike Bitcoin, it does not have a finite supply. Additionally, it is untraceable and focuses on the privacy aspects of cryptocurrencies, notably sacrificing scalability for this. Monero does not use any logs or servers to store transaction history.

However, that is also the reason why it is an obvious choice of "darknet" users.

Monero also solves the problems of scalability, anonymity, and constant supply.

Benefits of Monero Cryptocurrency:

Private: Nobody can see your balances by looking at the blockchain.

Secure: Irreversible cryptographic math-based security, which secures Monero transactions and wallets.

Untraceable: The Monero coins (XMR) cannot be traced back to the blockchain.

Decentralized: All the nodes or wallets are equally eligible to verify and mine Monero coins. Monero's mining algorithm protects against ASIC mining centralization.

Fungible: All the coins have the same market value irrespective of time or place. Each XMR is valued the same as the next XMR, with the ability to blacklist coins impossible.

Ripple

Ripple allows instant and nearly free global transactions that go beyond just cryptocurrency and work with fiat currency, including the traditional banking system.

When Ripple was first in development, it managed to attract venture capital support from Google and collected around US $50 million from banking institutions.

It has similar principles to Bitcoin; however, it's different than Bitcoin in the sense that the source code of Ripple's technology is privately-owned by the company and can't be verified by any outsider.

It is a popular cryptocurrency and many global banks use it for their settlement infrastructure. It consistently remains within the top five cryptocurrencies by market cap.

The critical difference between Ripple and Bitcoin are as follows:

1. Bitcoin and Ripple use a different method to reach network consensus. Bitcoin uses Proof-of-Work mining procedure while Ripple uses an iterative consensus process. As a result, Ripple is faster than Bitcoin. It only takes a few seconds to finalize transactions. It is also more energy efficient.

2. Bitcoin is a decentralized digital currency. Ripple is a transaction network that uses a digital currency called XRP.

3. The Bitcoin network tracks the movement of Bitcoins while the Ripple network can monitor information of any kind. As a result, Ripple can track account balances of any existing currency.

4. There is a finite number of Bitcoins (21 million). While XRPs are limited as well, they are substantially more (100 billion).

5. Bitcoin are awarded through mining. However, XRPs are given by the company OpenCoin (the company that developed Ripple). It aims to distribute them as widely, fairly, and diversely as possible.

6. Ripple allows for automated scripts, which means that it created something similar to contracts. For example, a script might say "if account A does not receive US$100 by November 1, then the money it received will automatically be returned to the original accounts."

Dash

The name 'dash' comes from a mix of the words 'digital' and 'cash'. It was originally known as Darkcoin, but later changed its name to Dash, due to 'dark' being associated with the dark web.

The idea of Dash is to make instant transactions, a feature that improves on Bitcoin's slow transaction time. Dash also functions as a Decentralized Autonomous Organization (DAO).

Dash claims that payments are confirmed in less than a second through its InstantSend feature. On the other hand, transactions through Bitcoin can take up to an hour to process and be confirmed.

To power its network, Dash uses two-tiered architecture. In the first tier, miners secure the network and write transactions to the blockchain.

In the second tier, there are 'masternodes', who work to enable Dash's advanced features.

In addition to instant transactions, Dash's other feature includes PrivateSend, which allows for private transactions.

Dash does some things better than Bitcoin. Some of the key ingredients Dash introduced that Bitcoin doesn't have:

Masternodes: Unlike Bitcoin, Dash introduced Masternodes to incentivize users with large Dash reserves to secure the network and add cool transactional features like InstantSend. Masternode operators invest 1,000 Dash to host a Masternode.

InstantSend: InstantSend uses the InstantX Masternode feature to send and confirm transactions in seconds. Bitcoin's block propagation takes an average of 10 minutes, and six confirmations for large purchases can take up to an hour.

PrivateSend: While Bitcoin transactions are pseudonymous and can be traced back to their users, Dash introduced PrivateSend transactions that allow users full privacy in their transactions.

Self-Sustainable Decentralized Governance: While Masternodes are incentivized and can govern the blockchain with 1 vote per Masternode, the Dash blockchain is also self-funded. A portion of each block (currently 10%) is allocated to the Network Development and Promotion Budget.

NEM

The New Economy Movement (NEM) provides much more than just a currency, (called XEM). Created in 2014, NEM has a fixed supply of 9 billion. NEM is not mined, it is harvested. When an account has 10,000 or more NEM, the money will naturally become vested by NEM's algorithm.

NEM has several unique features:

First, it is written in Java on an entirely new and different code base that is separate from Bitcoin's open source code.

Second, unlike Bitcoin, which is mined, NEM is harvested. Harvesting is very similar to mining, but the critical difference is that the generated block provides profits for multiple people.

Third, NEM also introduced several new features to the blockchain, including the Proof-of-Importance algorithm (which is used instead of a Proof-of-Work algorithm), encrypted messaging, and multi-signature accounts.

How does the Proof of Importance (POI) algorithm differ from POW?

The PoI in NEM is used to timestamp transactions. A user's importance is calculated by how many coins they have and the number of transactions they have engaged in.

Compared to PoS (Proof-of-Stake) algorithm, which requires a person to have a tremendous amount of coins to form a block, in PoI the volume of transactions and trust also are important factors.

The idea is to encourage users to actively carry out transactions rather than simply holding on to their coins. It has experienced rapid growth in 2017 since it became widely popular in Japan.

Ethereum Classic

Ethereum Classic exists on a parallel Ethereum platform. It has a large user community and consistently remains one of the top altcoins in terms of market cap. However, the question is – why are there two versions of the same platform?

The platform began over a disagreement. The Ethereum community disagreed over the way a technically legal theft of funds should be dealt with, causing the group to split. Most of the users wanted to change Ethereum's code to get their funds back.

Others decided that the code should not be meddled with and should be left untouched by third parties. The result was the minority creating Ethereum Classic, which today remains a strong altcoin. Ethereum Classic exists by the motto "Code is Law."

The majority elected to fork the blockchain to what is currently Ethereum, which is the 2nd largest cryptocurrency by market cap.

Zcash

Zcash is similar to Monero in the sense that it offers higher levels of privacy to its users. However, the critical difference is that with Zcash, transactions are not completely private; instead, they are shielded.

In other words, the details of the transactions, such as the users involved and the amount traded, is kept hidden by using a zero-knowledge proof algorithm. This allows users to exchange funds without uncovering their identities.

Zcash is a relatively new coin, as it was released in October 2016. Zcash's supply model is exceptionally similar to Bitcoin's, with a fixed and known issuance model that is cut in half approximately every four years.

Additionally, there is a maximum of 21 million units of both Zcash (ZEC) and Bitcoin (BTC) which will be mined over time.

Bitcoin Cash

Bitcoin Cash (BCH) was a split off from Bitcoin (BTC) after a minority of developers decided to implement an upgrade to the block size from Bitcoin's one megabyte to eight megabytes.

This increase in block size was aimed at countering Bitcoin's scalability problem (or how to accommodate more transactions per second) and the problems of declining speed and rising costs by the cryptocurrency.

Background of Blocks

To understand this, you need to know that Bitcoin transactions are grouped into blocks that are processed every 10 minutes. However, the amount of data that can be included in a given block is limited to one megabyte in Bitcoin. Therefore, the fees and time involved in transactions tend to rise parallel to the rise in transaction volume.

The Problem to Be Solved

As the transaction volumes continue to increase, developers began thinking of two ways to counter this problem of rising fees and time involved in transactions:

1. Organize items more efficiently, also called SegWit, where the critical items stay inside the block while the less important items remain outside the block.
2. Make the block size bigger, increasing the number of items that can fit in the block.

The Solution by Bitcoin Cash

Bitcoin Cash chose to make the block size bigger, from one megabyte to eight megabytes.

However, it is believed that Bitcoin Cash's solution to the problem is a short-term solution, as the higher block size of 8 megabytes becomes saturated, and thus, does not ensure a sustainable solution.

Whereas Bitcoin chose SegWit to implement into its blockchain, diverging the paths that both the currencies decided to assume.

Chapter 14

The Disadvantages of Cryptocurrency

Cryptocurrency has many benefits, such as its secure transactional properties and the decentralized environment. However, there are certain disadvantages of cryptocurrency that are bad for a casual user:

Losing Your Wallet

Just like in real life, you can lose your digital wallet. If you forget your login details or cannot access the platform, there is not much you can do. There are somewhat fewer options to retrieve the login details if you have lost them. There is also the risk of somebody stealing your credentials or personal keys which can lead to further losses.

Not Widely Accepted

There are not many companies or websites that accept Bitcoin as a method of payment. Thus, as a payment mechanism, you first have to find a service provider that receives it and only then can he use it.

Subject to Market Fluctuations

If you want to invest in cryptocurrency, you should keep in mind that it is dynamic and experiences an environment of changing market prices. While it can be used to buy and sell, it's also a commodity like oil.

It is best to look at Bitcoin as a long-term investment, rather than a quick way of making money.

Further, you must not get discouraged if the value suddenly drops and you lose a substantial amount, as the chances that you will recover it in the future are highly likely.

Irreversible

One of the cryptocurrency's fundamental properties is that you cannot reverse a transaction. Therefore, if you send it to the wrong person or you put an extra zero at the end of an address, the transaction cannot be reversed. It is a harsh reality, with no avenues of redressal.

Transactions Are Difficult to Trace

Cryptocurrency accounts cannot be linked to a physical and real address. While they can be traced to a digital wallet address, that does not allow for determining who is the account holder or the actual person behind a transaction.

This feature makes digital currency the perfect tool for criminal transactions and also one of the reasons why some governments declare cryptocurrency transactions illegal in their countries.

Chapter 15

Cryptocurrency Rules to Follow

When trading in the cryptocurrency world, there are some rules that you must follow to be safe and secure about your holdings and mitigate against potential fraud.

Due Diligence

Similar to opening a new bank account, you should thoroughly research the bank. Similarly, you must be thorough in you due diligence for a cryptocurrency exchange. You must do your research and be careful for a variety of potential fraudelent behaviors.

Apart from reading reviews, checking forums for any recent complaints or issues is a healthy practice. It is also worth searching through Google for 'exchange names' along with the word 'scam' and observe the results that are returned.

The most reliable sources for any information on cryptocurrencies are Reddit, GitHub or BitcoinTalk. If you come across a complaint or the same one repeatedly pops up everywhere, then it is probably a malicious attack rather than a genuine criticism.

Customer Service

Customer service is an essential aspect of the cryptocurrency world as it is critical at times due to the transactions occurring in an unregulated environment.

You can check the customer service desk of a cryptocurrency exchange by sending them a query or opening a support ticket. If they do not get

Michael Gonzalez

back to you within 24 hours, then there is a problem with the customer service.

Exchange Details

The exchange should be as transparent as possible. You should check the country of origin of the exchange and details about how long the exchange has been in service.

In the past, cryptocurrency exchanges were created mainly in tax havens. Nowadays, they are moving to major financial centers like San Francisco and London.

Fees

You must check the deposit, withdrawal and transfer fees of the exchange before joining. The reliable exchanges will provide these details in the 'Fees' or 'Help' section. It is common that exchanges have higher fees for credit card transactions.

Irreversible Transactions

It is important to note that cryptocurrency transactions are irreversible, unlike bank card transactions. Therefore, it is important to double check transaction address and transaction amounts before sending the funds to a recipient address.

Chapter 16

Differences between Investing and Trading Bitcoin

It is important to note the difference between investing and trading cryptocurrency when entering into the world of cryptocurrency. To a beginner, cryptocurrency might seem like a gold mine, where they can merely mine using the click of a button.

Investing vs. Trading Bitcoin

Investing is a long-term undertaking, which features a portfolio of cryptocurrencies, chosen with risk factors and investing objectives in mind. In most cases, cryptocurrency investors are indifferent to price volatility and do not give up on the investment easily.

Investment also means holding the cryptocurrency until there is a perfect moment to sell, which can sometimes take years and are impossible to predict.

In contrast, Bitcoin trading is a short-term endeavor, where you join the market, stay in a trade for a few months and move on as soon as the price reaches its peak.

Bitcoin traders are known to be price-sensitive and for abandoning the market when it becomes unprofitable.

Is it Better to Invest or Trade?

The choice between investing and trading depends on many parameters, such as experience, available assets, and personality. Investing in a cryptocurrency can start from a minuscule amount, and can keep on increasing with time and expertise.

It is also a long-term undertaking, which eventually might lead to accumulating a significant sum of money. You must come prepared to the market with a patient mindset, as long-term holds come with nerve-wracking volatility.

Trading, on the other hand, is meant for those who know the cryptocurrency market extensively and are not afraid of losing. The constant fluctuations can be an exhilarating experience for traders, but it can also scare away those who do not know how to deal with it.

Chapter 17

How to Choose Cryptocurrency to Invest

There are hundreds of coins listed on numerous exchanges, and the number keeps on growing. However, not many of them end up gaining traction.

In the beginning, you may start investing in Bitcoin or Ethereum, as these are the two biggest cryptocurrencies on the market, sold by almost all of the exchanges.

However, the real deal starts when evaluating altcoins, as there are so many of them out there that it becomes difficult to differentiate between legitimate coins and scams.

The key to investing in altcoins is to determine if a coin is innovative or it has been created as a joke. Understanding the financial potential of the project and its potential of being a scam are vital. You must look at specific aspects while choosing which cryptocurrency to invest in.

However, there are cases where some of them might seem a great coin, but in reality, might not be. Sometimes revelations about specific cryptocurrencies don't happen until months or years after their ICOs, leaving investors in financial ruin.

These are the rules you have to look at while assessing a coin's classification:

- Track on a daily basis

- CoinMarketCap is one of the most reliable and trivial platforms to use to check current crypto prices, featuring all 1000+ cryptocurrencies.

Market Cap

Market capitalization is the market value of cryptocurrency's outstanding coins. This figure is discovered through taking the coin price and multiplying it by the total number of coins in the circulating supply.

For example, if in the past 24 hours Bitcoin was trading at $6,900 and had 16,000,000 coins in circulation, then the market capitalization is $110,400,000,000 ($6900*16, 000,000 coins). It's that simple.

A common misconception about trading cryptocurrencies is that the higher the price, the higher the value of the coin. The truth is that cryptocurrency price alone cannot indicate the real worth of the coin.

What's the Problem With This?

Consider the picture below which shows a list of top cryptocurrencies as listed on Coinmarketcap.com. Carefully study the values under the price column of the chart. Now, look at the values under the "Market Cap" column. What do you notice?

First, the cryptocurrencies are listed in descending order starting with the one with the highest market cap, all the way down to the one with the smallest market cap. This is because when it comes to assessing the worth of a cryptocurrency, the market cap is currently the best metric for doing so.

Looking at the picture above, Ripple, for example, has over $8 billion invested in it while more than $3 billion is invested in Litecoin. A quick look at their prices reveal a striking difference — Ripple is priced at $0.2115 whereas the price of Litecoin is $64.19.

The stark contrasting difference between the Ripple price and the Litecoin price is a result of the difference in supply. Crypto prices are affected by supply, and all cryptocurrencies have varying quantities. In the example above, Ripple has a coin supply of more than 38 billion XRP while the Litecoin supply is over 53 million LTC.

Litecoin is $64.19, yet cheaper than Ripple, which is priced at just $0.2115. This implies that Litecoin offers higher rewards than Ripple, but carries higher risks.

When investing, you need to consider the risk and reward ratio of any cryptocurrency -- coins with small caps have a higher potential to increase in value than the ones with large caps, but they also pose higher risks.

The best investment strategy for cryptocurrency is one that focuses on diversifying the portfolio such that a small percentage is committed to smaller cap coins and the more substantial portion allocated to larger market cap coins.

Chapter 18

How to Transfer Crypto from Coinbase to Binance

While Coinbase is an excellent exchange for purchasing the top coins such as Bitcoin (BTC) or Ethereum (ETH), it doesn't allow for buying most altcoins such as Ripple (XRP), Monero (XMR), or NEO (NEO). In that case, you'll need to purchase these coins on a different exchange by transferring BTC, ETH or LTC from Coinbase to the exchange you would like to use.

One popular and secure exchange that you can use is Binance. Binance enables you to invest in emerging cryptocurrencies by purchasing the coins/tokens that are listed on the Binance exchange. Because of its large trading volume, Binance offers better liquidity and efficiency, making it an outstanding exchange. Binance even offers discounts on transaction fees (trading, withdrawal and listing fees) if you pay in Binance coin (BNB), their native cryptocurrency.

How do you transfer crypto from Coinbase to Binance?

Before diving into the steps to transfer coins from Coinbase to Binance, it is important to note that Binance is primarily an exchange that does not support fiat money deposits. This means you need to buy Bitcoin at Coinbase and then transfer the funds to Binance to exchange Bitcoin for the altcoins that you want.

Below is a step-by-step guide showing how to transfer crypto from your Coinbase account to your Binance account.

Step 1: Log into your Coinbase and at the top of your screen click on Accounts. If you're using the mobile app then Accounts will be at the bottom of your screen.

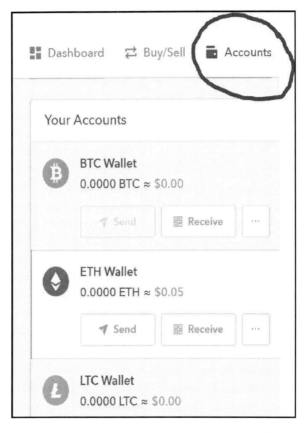

Step 2: Choose the cryptocurrency you want to send from your wallets. In our case, it is **BTC Wallet.**

Step 3: Click **Send**. Now a screen will pop up prompting you to enter the Binance address where the funds will be sent to. It will look like this.

If you're on a mobile device, go to the top right-hand side of your screen and tap on the small paper airplane icon to open the pop-up box. Next, enter the amount you want to send and click **Continue.**

The funds won't be sent until you provide your Binance deposit address. To get this address, go to Binance and log into your Binance account. If you don't have a Binance account yet, you can register for free following a few simple steps.

Here's how to register.

Go to Binance official website (https://www.binance.com/).

Next, click on the **Register** button at the top right-hand side of your screen.

Enter your email address and password to register. Make sure you use your actual email address since you will be asked to verify this email address.

Confirm your email by clicking on the email link sent to the email address provided during the registration. Congratulations, your account is activated.

Next, login to your account and complete the Two-Factor Authentication (2FA) process to protect your funds and investment. 2FA basically adds another level of security in addition to your password. You can choose either Google Authentication or SMS Authentication to enable 2FA.

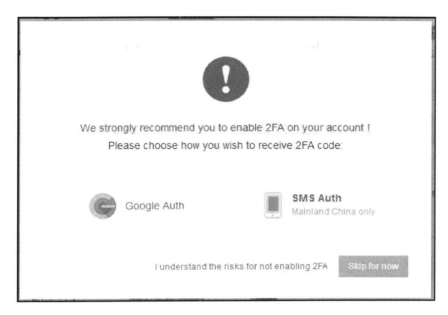

Once you've had your account protected, you are now free to transfer funds from Coinbase to Binance. You're doing exceptionally well. Now let's move to the next step.

Step 4: On the top right-hand side of your Binance account, select **Funds** then **Deposits.** If you're on mobile you can find Funds at the bottom of the screen.

Step 5: Type BTC and select BTC-Bitcoin once it appears on the coin box and then get the **BTC Deposit Address**.

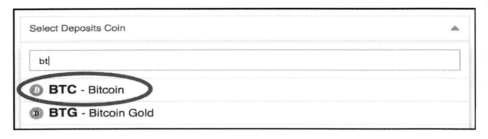

Step 6: Now what you have to do is copy this address and then jump back into your Coinbase account and paste it into **Recipient** field.

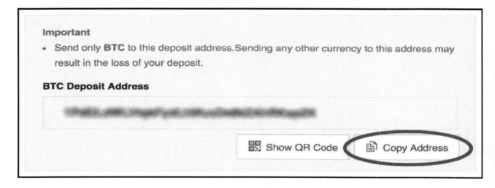

Step 7: Next, on Coinbase paste the address (which you just copied from Binance) into the **Enter the BTC Address** field.

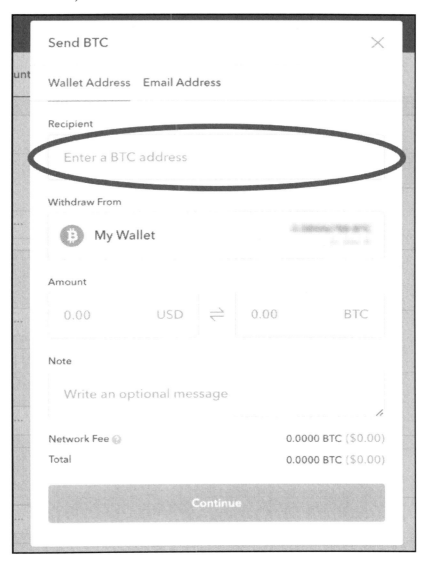

Step 8: Select the amount that you want to send. Lastly, click **Continue** and confirm all the details of the transaction. On mobile devices, just add the address you've just received from Binance and then tap **Send**.

That's it. Your funds are now on the way to the Binance exchange. It may take a while (15-30 minutes or longer) to see the funds deposited on your Binance account. You may check the status of your transaction under the **Transactions** page on Coinbase.

Once the funds are successfully deposited in your Binance account, you can start trading.

Chapter 19

How to Transfer Profits from Binance back to Coinbase

After depositing bitcoins on Binance and trading altcoins, you may want to cash out or transfer the profits back to your Coinbase wallet. In fact, you can withdraw part or all of your cryptocurrency holdings.

The walkthrough below takes you through the steps of withdrawing on Binance and transferring profits back to Coinbase account.

Step 1: On your Binance account, go to the Funds button located on the upper-right corner of the screen as you did when depositing Bitcoin. Select the Withdrawals option or tap Withdrawals if you're on the mobile app.

Step 2: Before you proceed, Binance will ask you to set up your two-factor authentication if you have not done so. Make sure you complete the 2FA authentication process. Simply go to Google Authenticator App to retrieve the code then head back to Binance and type in the authentication code in the box within the confirmation code.

Step 3: Click **Select Withdrawal Coin** then type BTC and select BTC-Bitcoin once it appears.

Step 4: Now, enter your Coinbase wallet's address under the BTC **Withdrawal Address** box. If you're on the mobile app, scan the QR code of the wallet by tapping on the QR button on the right-hand side of the address tab. You'll need to generate the QR code on Coinbase prior to this.

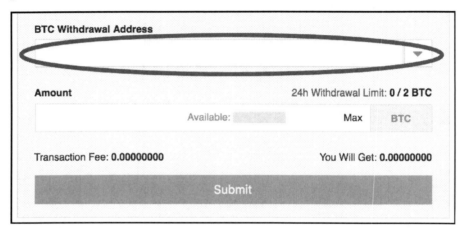

Alternatively, you can get the address by going to Coinbase and then the **Accounts** tab. Next, click **Receive** on your Bitcoin wallet to get the address.

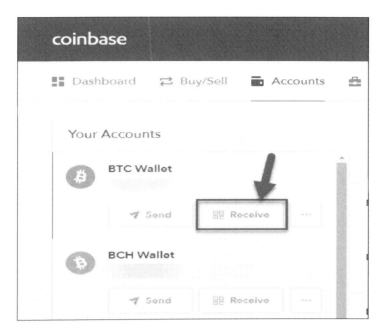

Copy this address by clicking **Copy Address** (or you can copy and paste manually).

Step 5: Now, go back to your Binance account and paste the address into the **BTC Withdrawal Address** field. On Binance, enter the amount you want to transfer to Coinbase in the denomination box. If you want to withdraw all of your funds, select **MAX** (or 100%) on the right-hand side of the box.

Step 6: Once you're satisfied with your selection click **Withdraw** to continue. Your Bitcoin will be transferred to your Coinbase wallet in 10-15 minutes. To view the status of your transfers, go to the Transaction History page. On Coinbase, you can view it on your **Accounts** page.

Chapter 20

How to Sell and Transfer Profits back to Bank Account or Wallet

Since Bitcoin cannot be withdrawn into a bank directly, the only way to take your profits out of Coinbase is first to sell your Bitcoin. That means you'll need to sell or "cash out" your bitcoins for your local currency and have the profits deposited into your linked bank account.

The following steps illustrate how to sell Bitcoin and withdraw money from Coinbase.

Step 1: Log in to your Coinbase account and navigate to the Sells page. If you're on a mobile device, go to the top left of your screen and tap the menu icon to open the navigation bar. Then select Sell.

Step 2: Enter the amount you want to sell.

Step 3: Next, select the wallet you want to sell from. In this case, it is the BTC Wallet.

Step 4: Choose the account you wish to deposit your proceeds into. On the "Deposit To" tab, select either your linked bank account or your USD Wallet.

Step 5: Once you've selected the account to deposit your funds into, you'll automatically be taken back to the Sells page. From there, either input the Bitcoin (BTC) amount or its dollar value. If you want to sell all of your Bitcoin balance, click the "Sell Max" button, but remember to factor in transaction fees.

Step 6: A confirmation page will now pop up showing the rate, time of arrival, withdrawal method and applicable fees. If you're satisfied with the order, click Sell Bitcoin Instantly to finalize the transaction.

It is important to note that it may take up to a week for the funds to be deposited into your bank account. However, if you are transferring funds from Coinbase to your USD Wallet, the transaction process is instant.

Chapter 21

Bitcoin Arbitraging

One good thing about online exchanges is that they offer varying prices of Bitcoin since the markets are not directly connected. This is a wonderful opportunity that can be explored in a trading method known as arbitrage trading.

Bitcoin arbitrage is a type of margin trading in which you buy Bitcoin on an exchange where the price is lower, and sell them at a higher price on another exchange.

For example:

Suppose we buy 10 bitcoins on Coinbase at the price of $9250 each, and subsequently, we sell them on Binance at the rate of $9258 each. The result is we make $8 per Bitcoin.

Here's a breakdown to explain Bitcoin arbitrage:

Number of bitcoins bought on Coinbase = 10

Price of each Bitcoin = $9250

Total Price $9250*10 = $92500

Number of Bitcoin sold on Binance = 10

Price of each Bitcoin = $9258

Total price = $9258*10 = $92580

Total profit = $92580-$92500 = $80

As you can see, moving funds from one exchange to another via arbitrage is a great way to make profits trading crypto.

However, Bitcoin arbitrage isn't that simple. Some fees are involved with it such as fiat deposit fees, fiat withdrawal fees, Bitcoin deposit fees, Bitcoin withdrawal fees, and transaction costs. In addition, the exchange rates might change while each of the transactions (buying and selling) is still processing.

Nevertheless, Bitcoin arbitrage can be carried out profitably in two ways.

The first way involves growing the spread (the difference between buy and sell values) a bit larger to capitalize on any price increases.

The second profitable way is to set strict guidelines for when, and how to engage in Bitcoin arbitrage. This can be accomplished by the use of custom arbitrage bots or through hiring an arbitrage professional to do it for you. An arbitrage professional can help you monitor the markets closely and place simultaneous trades to ensure you optimize arbitraging.

Chapter 22

Bitcoin Technical Analysis - Understanding Bitcoin Price Charts

Before taking the plunge into buying Bitcoin, it is crucial to understand Bitcoin price charts and risks. Understanding trading terms help in determining the amount of Bitcoin you hold when converted to your local currency. It also helps to strategize on when to hold or sell bitcoins.

This chapter looks into the Bitcoin trading basics to help you analyze price charts and trade bitcoins more profitably.

What is Bitcoin's Current Price?

The current Bitcoin price is the latest price of Bitcoin determined using an average from major global exchanges. The best place to find live and the most accurate price of Bitcoin is Coinbase or other popular exchanges such as Binance, Bitfinex, and BTC-E.

Besides understanding Bitcoin's current price, you may want to know how the prices will behave in the future.

How Bitcoin's Price Trends Are Predicted

It is risky to forecast price movements of Bitcoin due to the volatile nature of cryptocurrency markets. The market is changing so fast that it is extremely difficult to predict where Bitcoin's price will go next.

However, there are two main approaches that traders use to predict price trends in Bitcoin; fundamental analysis and technical analysis.

Fundamental Analysis

Fundamental analysis predicts price trends by examining the underlying forces of the Bitcoin economy. Fundamental analysis is undoubtedly the most vital to evaluating the real value of Bitcoin. It looks at various factors that influence the supply and demand for Bitcoin. For example, Bitcoin's demand is affected by user adoption, trading and transaction activity.

In regards to the supply of Bitcoin, the market is more straightforward. The total number of units set by the Bitcoin protocol is 21 million, and more than 80 percent of bitcoins are in circulation today. Also, only the Bitcoin protocol can determine the rate of new supply.

Technical Analysis

Technical analysis attempts to predict the direction of Bitcoin's price by looking into past market data, trade volumes, and historical price charts.

Fundamental Analysis vs. Technical Analysis

The difference between fundamental analysis and technical analysis is that while fundamental analysis focuses on evaluating the economic, financial and other key variables to determine Bitcoin's true value, technical analysis is more interested in looking at Bitcoin's price movements for more informed trading decisions.

To conduct technical analysis on the Bitcoin price, you must look at a simple Bitcoin price chart that is easy to read and understand. These kinds of charts can be found on major exchanges like Coinbase or Binance.

Below is a simple price chart that displays prices as a line.

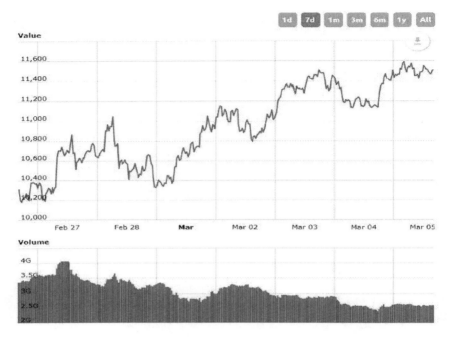

This simple price chart helps you to get a quick overview of Bitcoin prices based on current trends. The price line is drawn using closing prices for a specific period such as one day, one week or one month.

Because of the limited data provided on these charts, they are not the best for drawing definitive conclusions. Hence the need for candlestick charts.

Candlestick Charts

A candlestick chart is a type of technical analysis chart used to display price movements of Bitcoin. They belong to the OHLC (open-high, low-close bars) family of price charts.

The figure below represents a candlestick chart. It is the most ubiquitous type of chart used by Bitcoin traders.

Unlike simple charts that display just the closing price, candlestick charts show more data. This data, which often is displayed in candle-like bars, represents the opening price, closing price, highest, and lowest prices over a given period.

In addition, the color of the "candles" indicates whether the closing price was higher than the opening price. A green bar (up-bar) indicates that the closing price was higher than the opening price while a red bar (down-bar) indicates that the closing price was lower than the opening price.

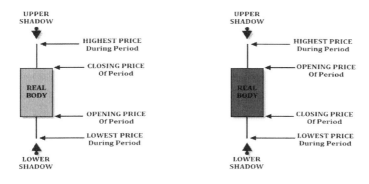

Candlesticks build patterns that predict price direction.

Candlestick patterns offer traders an outstanding way to gain insights into Bitcoin markets to maximize performance. They assist in determining whether the candle's spread is broad or narrow (the difference between high and low prices) and to check for high-odds bullish (rising prices) or bearish (falling prices) outcomes.

Traders rely on candlestick patterns to predict both the price direction and momentum of Bitcoin. They are highly reliable because they allow for short-term and long-term profit opportunities.

As a beginner trader, you need to spend time reading Bitcoin price charts to gain insights into how Bitcoin's price is developing on a daily basis. With time, you will start noticing specific behaviors on the charts, especially trends in price direction. It is at this point that you need to begin conducting technical price analysis to draw meaningful conclusions.

How to perform technical analysis and identify trends in bitcoin price charts

As discussed above, trends play an important role in trading. Traders rely on patterns in price data to make decisions on whether to sell or buy Bitcoin.

So how do you identify a trend on a Bitcoin price chart?

Consider the Bitcoin price chart shown in the figure below. Notice how prices at times seem to move along imaginary lines irrespective of which time frame you choose to look at.

The lines you see in the chart above represent "trend lines". A closer look at the price chart shows two trend lines, an upper and a lower trend line. The price of Bitcoin seems to be moving back and forth between the two trend lines. Traders call this the "trend channel."

When it comes to technical price analysis, trends are often divided into shorter segments, which are further divided into even shorter segments. Another important aspect of price trends is that they are highly fractal in nature. That is, they will appear similar no matter what timeframe you choose to view them from.

Drawing Trend Lines

To understand how the Bitcoin price is changing, you need to draw trend lines and channels. Online exchanges like Coinstackr provide traders with an interactive platform to draw on Bitcoin charts. You can draw either uptrends or downtrends.

Uptrends generally describe the price movement of Bitcoin when the overall direction is upward while downtrends describe the price movement when the overall direction is downwards.

How to Draw Uptrends

In an uptrend, each successive candlestick's highs and lows are above the ones found earlier in the trend.

The first thing to know about drawing trend lines is that you need to identify at least two points in the chart to start a trend line.

To draw an uptrend, start the trend line at one end of a given trend's lows and then draw it to one of the next higher lows. The line will extend to the right or left depending on the tool used. In addition, the blue moving average indicator on the chart helps you draw the line at a good angle.

Now, move the line around a bit and adjust the angle so it touches the trend's price lows as accurately as possible. Note that the trends line never perfectly fit so you will see some candles piercing the line.

How to Draw Downtrend Lines

In a downtrend line, each successive high and low of price candlesticks are lower than the ones found before it in the trend.

To draw a price downtrend, identify two main points at which to start drawing the line. Start the trend line at the upper high and draw it to one of the next upper lows. Adjust the line as accurately as possible to ensure you get more touches without cutting through the body of the candle. Do not try to force the trend line. If it doesn't fit the chart then it isn't valid and therefore not worth using to analyze trade.

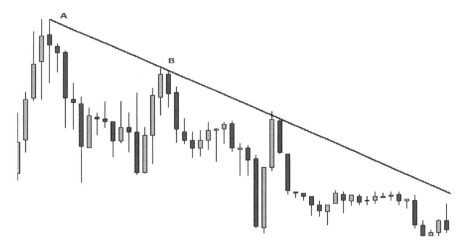

Using Trends In Bitcoin Trading

Trends can be used to identify buying and selling opportunities that occur within the Bitcoin market. An uptrend in the price presents an opportunity to buy into Bitcoin and make a profit.

However, money can also be made when the Bitcoin price falls (downtrend) in a trading strategy called short-selling. The ability to spot a downtrend can save you money. A downtrend in price tells you to get out the bitcoins you previously purchased so that the falling price doesn't erode all the profits.

Short-selling is a technique that traders use to trade a downtrend. It involves trading Bitcoin when a correction to the upside develops. Plan short-selling during that corrective wave, based on the assumption that the price will have another impulse wave lower.

It is worth noting that while trends can be useful in trading, it is not advisable to use them as the only factor in a trading decision. Always check with other indicators such as support and resistance levels, price action patterns and volume analysis to make sure the trend you're following is not going to break and lose you money.

Further, be careful to look for higher and lower timeframe trends. That way, you can be sure that the prices in the uptrend on higher timeframe are not revealing a downtrend instead.

Chapter 23

Fundamental Analysis

When it comes to assessing the fundamental or underlying value of Bitcoin, technical analysis alone is never enough. While technical analysis can help in making price predictions, it does not help with predicting transactional demands.

Fundamental analysis entails the evaluation of Bitcoin viability by looking at various factors that influence the supply and demand for Bitcoin. We perform fundamental analysis to ensure we make the best-informed investments decisions and are on top of our game.

There are fewer metrics available to analyze, making it quite challenging to perform fundamental analysis for Bitcoin. Unlike traditional stocks that have financial statements to evaluate, no such data exists for bitcoin.

Of course, many different strategies have proven to be the most effective for evaluating Bitcoin's value. Bitcoin traders consider both qualitative and quantitative factors when performing fundamental analysis of bitcoin.

In regards to the fundamental analysis of Bitcoin, an analyst would look at the trading volume of the cryptocurrency as a quantitative factor. Also integrated into the fundamental analysis are qualitative factors such as Bitcoin's future potential as a widely adopted common medium of exchange. That means, Bitcoin's fundamental analysis not only assesses its current value, but also the opportunities it presents in the future.

Bitcoin Supply

The total supply of Bitcoin is fixed at 21 million units. This number represents the total volume of Bitcoin, but it also places Bitcoin in a unique category as a currency. That is, Bitcoin has a fixed and predictable total supply volume.

Besides the Bitcoin units that have already been mined, there is also a small volume of "lost Bitcoin'. These are bitcoins stored in digital wallets and whose owners have either lost or discarded the drives containing the keys required to access their Bitcoin. As a result, these bitcoins will never move.

Bitcoin Demand

The forces of supply and demand play a huge role in determining Bitcoin's value. Trading volume and transaction availability determine the demand for Bitcoin. User adoption rates are measured by looking at the number of units that are trading at a given period as well as transaction availability.

Essentially, as people continue to adopt Bitcoin as a means to transfer monetary value, the more it becomes accepted as a standard medium of exchange. Widespread adoption of Bitcoin as a medium of exchange has been slow but steady.

Although there has been staggering growth in transaction volume over the last few years, several stores and e-commerce platforms have already started accepting Bitcoin as a form of payment. Today, Amazon, PayPal, Dell, Shopify, Overstock.com and Microsoft all accept Bitcoin.

In regards to transaction availability, the total number of Bitcoin transactions has soared and have demonstrated an upward trend. Currently, over 33,000 Bitcoin transactions are completed daily, and that number is growing.

To assess Bitcoin's worth, transaction availability and trading volume are crucial indicators you need to look at.

Economic Events

Since Bitcoin's asset class is undefined at this point, its price can also be impacted by global economic events. These economic events must, therefore, be factored into fundamental Bitcoin analysis. Even if the event is unrelated to the currency directly, it can still have a profound impact.

Related economic events can vary from major hacks on popular Bitcoin exchanges to government legislative decisions and pre-announcements concerning cryptocurrencies.

In pre-announcements, for example, traders usually take advantage of upcoming news concerning Bitcoin to buy the currency before the report is announced and capitalize on any price increase. This is normally helped by the increase in Bitcoin's price and trading volume in the build-up to good news.

Events that appear unrelated to Bitcoin can also have an impact on the future price of the currency. For example, it has been demonstrated that global economic crises like the ongoing economic financial and economic crisis in Greece have directly resulted in the increasing price of Bitcoin.

Using Fundamental Analysis in Bitcoin Trading

Leveraging the insights obtained from fundamental analysis can provide Bitcoin traders with an in-depth understanding of the price of the cryptocurrency, which ultimately helps in making better informed and profitable trading decisions.

The only problem with fundamental analysis is that it is speculative and theoretical in nature. It is more concerned with the hypothetical worth of the currency instead of its true value at any given point in time. Bitcoin traders balance out this speculative element of fundamental analysis by combining the insights it offers with those of technical analysis to gain a comprehensive and balanced perspective on Bitcoin price.

For example, suppose we perform a fundamental analysis of Bitcoin and come to the conclusion that it is currently overpriced. A good trader will spot this opportunity and begin to work out the optimal time to sell. In that case, we employ technical analysis to gain insights into a profitable exit price.

Fundamental analysis can also prove useful when buying Bitcoin. By assessing the recent volume and price data of Bitcoin, you can leverage technical analysis to calculate the best time to buy, which can then be balanced with fundamental analysis to confirm the decision.

Coin Burn

Coin burn in cryptocurrencies refers to sending native cryptocurrency to a public address that is verifiable, invalid, and unspendable, and which cannot be spent or used. By doing so, the coins are taken out of circulation entirely because they cannot be used anymore.

To demonstrate to investors evidence that these cryptocurrencies have been burned, a method called "Proof-of-Burn" was developed.

Proof-of-Burn in Cryptocurrencies

Proof-of-Burn is a method of distributed consensus that works much in the same way as proof-of-work or proof-of-stake. This method provides empirical and untampered evidence showing that cryptocurrencies have been burned, that is, they have been sent to a verifiably unspendable address.

The idea is that miners or participants are willing to undergo short-term losses for long-term investments by burning the native cryptocurrency. Participants usually get special privileges of mining blocks in weight of the coins that they have burnt. Additionally, proof-of-burn consumes no resources other than the underlying assets burned.

Reasons for Cryptocurrency Coin Burns

Long-Term Commitment

Coins are usually burned to encourage long-term commitment on a project. This is purposely done to create an economic scarcity so that token/coin HODlers benefit from it. As a result, the price stability of the coin is boosted due to high demand and because long-term holders are unlikely to sell or spend their coins.

Getting Rid of Unsold Coins/Tokens

During the ICO sales, the remaining coins that are not sold are burned to discourage companies from selling them on the market and making a profit. This ensures that only the value received from the actual sale is used to develop the product the company is working on.

Paying for Transaction Fees

Proof-of-Burn can also be used to pay for transaction fees. Ripple, for instance, uses this method to help drive up the price of the token. For every Ripple transaction, a minuscule amount of that transaction is burned.

Creating New Tokens or Coins

Another reason why cryptocurrencies are burned is that a newly created token has value because of the burn. When developers create new cryptocurrency, interested parties invest in the project by sending Bitcoin to an unspendable address. The cryptocurrency that the investors receive has value because of the demand, and a similar value is transferred to the developers.

Counterparty used proof-of-burn to avoid pre-mining or ICO. The developers asked investors to send Bitcoin (BTC) in an unusable or unspendable address, and in exchange for these BTC, Counterparty tokens (XCP) were generated on the Bitcoin blockchain.

Rebranding

Blockchain branding or rebranding is an emerging marketing discipline in the cryptocurrency world in which already established projects change their corporate identity by highlighting and emphasizing their blockchain developers' skills and specialties as well as telling consumers what they are offering, therefore attracting the right people.

The goal is to create a different identity for a project and appeal to the targeted audience to grow a stronger community. Rebranding involves changing the project's logo, front-end design, or giving it a new name to make the platform more appealing and resonate with users tastes and experiences.

Lisk, for example, had to base their rebranding on a vision to provide a blockchain platform that can be used by a wider audience, not just developers.

Blockchain rebranding is vital because it helps brands attract customers by not only saying they work with blockchains but by also communicating what their purpose is in a better fashion. Indeed, some traditional companies have seen their share price rocket when they rebrand to a blockchain company, perhaps suggesting that the disruptive potential of blockchain is real.

What is a Fork in Blockchain and Why Does Forking Happen?

In a blockchain protocol, a fork is a technical event that occurs when participants have protocol versions that are different from the primary one and need to agree on standard rules.

In its most basic, a fork occurs when a blockchain diverges into two potential paths forward based on the network's transaction history or a new rule in deciding what makes a transaction valid. As a result, the participants of the blockchain have to decide on one path at the expense of the other.

For example, if two miners discover a block at nearly the same time, this uncertainty is resolved by adding the subsequent blocks to one, making it the longest chain while the other block is abandoned (orphaned) by the network.

Forks can also occur when developers seek to change the protocol that helps determine whether a transaction is valid or not. This implies that a block that contains invalid transactions is ignored by the blockchain and the miner who found that block loses out on a block reward.

Hard Fork

A hard fork is a protocol change that works in parallel with the old protocol. It introduces new rules that are not in synchrony with the old ones. What happens is that nodes that continue running the old protocol will see the new transactions as invalid, forcing miners to switch over to the new protocol to mine valid blocks.

The only problem with hard forks is that it can cause a split amongst the community if there's no agreement over the rules.

Soft Fork

A soft fork is a protocol change, but with backward compatibility. A soft fork doesn't necessarily require miners to upgrade their blockchain versions to the new protocol but the blocks they mine with non-upgraded nodes will be rejected by the soft fork. That being said, a soft fork still requires a majority of hash power in the network for it to be successful, or else it becomes the shortest chain and gets orphaned by the network.

Partnerships

For blockchain projects seeking to raise funds through ICOs, strategic partnerships are key to attracting enthusiasm and legitimacy to the project. When assessing the potential of a new or established ICO, it advisable to check if the project has attracted strategic partnerships with high-profile players or tech-savvy employees.

Credible ICOs announce and publicize partnerships early in the development phase. Partnerships can take several forms, including banks, technology partners, exchanges, venture capital, retail/ enterprise partners, government institutions and channel partners. In addition, projects with significant resources, stable vision, a stellar team of advisors and community backing will likely stand the test of time.

Roadmaps

Roadmaps are about the project's concreteness, feasibility, vision, maturity, and future. Investments in cryptocurrency assets shouldn't be limited to when the tokens hit the exchange, but demonstrate a little more concern about what happens a year or even five years from now. An ICO without a roadmap has no direction and should not be trusted. There's no excuse for a project not to outline specific indicators that will prove to its investors that everything they promise is on schedule.

In essence, the roadmap and its content have a way of helping investors know when to be more involved in the project and when to steer clear. Some projects even mislead investors by spreading a single activity of the development over many weeks and even months or years, when in reality that activity can be achieved within a shorter time frame. The deception makes it look like they will be busy for an extended period and it would be good to make a stake for a long-term investment.

When analyzing an ICO roadmap, look through the information carefully and check if the claims are bogus or if they can be achieved based on what the final product will be like.

The best project roadmaps are clear, outlined and well-structured with indicators about quarterly prospective goals, alpha, beta and final versions of the platform as well as a broader, long-term vision.

Whitepaper

Before buying any tokens or investing in an ICO, it is important to read the project's whitepaper. Whitepapers are authoritative guides that inform investors about a problem that exists in the market and how the new blockchain project solves it. The goal of a whitepaper is to convince potential investors that the project has a legitimate business idea that will succeed.

The document also presents the development team, advisors, and partners behind the project. When investors see credible and experienced people supporting the ICO, they are more likely to invest in it.

An excellent whitepaper includes the following the following information:

- The vision of the project

- The technology

- The market problem that will be solved

- How the tokens will be distributed

- Timeline of milestones that the company aims to   reach

- The core team and its record

Long-term investors review each element of a whitepaper carefully to determine the long-term survival and growth of the company. Always look for an ICO that has a clear vision and developers who are passionate about their goals.

Differences Between Coins and Tokens

While most coins do not function as a currency or medium of exchange, all coins and tokens are regarded as cryptocurrencies. Cryptocurrencies are commonly categorized into two -- altcoins and tokens.

Altcoins

Altcoins or coins are cryptocurrencies that are alternatives to Bitcoin. The majority of altcoins are Bitcoin forks, that is, they are built using Bitcoin's open-sourced, original protocol with small changes to its underlying codes, resulting in the creation of an entirely new coin. Examples of altcoins that are variants of Bitcoin's code include Litecoin, Peercoin, Bitcoin Cash, Namecoin, and Aurora coin.

Other altcoins that are not derived from Bitcoin's open source protocol include Ripple, Etherem, NEO, Counterparty, among others. One thing about altcoins is that they all possess their own independent blockchain, where transactions relating to their native coins occur.

Tokens

Tokens are usually created on top of other blockchains and are a representation of a particular digital asset or utility. Tokens can represent literally any digital asset ranging from fungible and tradeable assets to commodities or even cryptocurrencies.

Tokens are created on a blockchain through smart contracts. They are always created and distributed through an Initial Coin Offering (ICO) as a way to source funds to finance the project.

As we conclude this chapter, it is important to note that in the world of cryptocurrency trading, knowledge is power. The more knowledgeable you are in Bitcoin, the more successful your trading strategy will be.

Chapter 24

Initial Coin Offerings (ICOs)

Blockchain technology has given rise to a new method of raising capital, known as Initial Coin Offerings (ICOs). Since the start of 2016, the number of blockchain-based startups seeking funding through ICO financing model has grown tremendously. We've also seen a rapid rise in the amount of capital raised through ICOs.

The meteoric rise of ICO's is largely attributed to the Bitcoin revolution. Since its inception, Bitcoin has increased in value exponentially as more people continue to accept the digital currency as a credible medium of exchange. While Bitcoin enjoys widespread adoption, awareness around blockchain technology and cryptocurrency has increased. As a result, the marketplace has seen more cryptocurrencies and tokens launched through the Initial Coin Offering financing model.

ICOs have become the fastest growing crowdfunding mechanism for funding blockchain projects. So, what makes ICOs so powerful in raising funds for new projects?

First, let's look at what an ICO is.

What are ICOs?

ICOs are a form of financing that involves the selling of cryptocurrency tokens in exchange for funding via another cryptocurrency, in most cases in Bitcoin or Ethereum.

ICOs work in a similar fashion as crowdfunding campaigns except that digital tokens are offered in place of shares of equity or copy of a product.

In an ICO sale, companies developing new blockchain-based products turn to the cryptocurrency community to crowdsource the purchase and usage of their tokens instead of looking to the traditional angel or venture investors to exchange capital for equity.

Since ICOs are not intended to be security offerings, they don't confer ownership in the underlying blockchain platform. Instead, they are offered as "utility tokens." This means that the tokens have some functionalities and rights attached to them—the people who use the platform pay for the services offered in the token.

A typical example of a utility token in use today is the Ether token. Ether (ETH) is the primary cryptocurrency of the Ethereum platform. On the Ethereum network, the transactions fees paid in Ether are called "gas," which is a derivate of Ether.

As you can see, Ether is a utility token that confers rights to access and pay for computational and transactional services on the Ethereum network. Further, just like Bitcoin, Ether can be bought, sold and traded on major exchanges.

Why Invest in ICOs?

ICOs offer an excellent opportunity for cryptocurrency holders and traders to diversify their holdings using the cryptocurrency itself, without taking the money out into fiat currency (offline bank-based dollars). With ICOs, anyone can become an investor with little risk as a consequence, as ICOs offer considerably higher returns than traditional investments. However, trading ICOs can also be very risky, as prices of tokens are incredibly volatile. Before investing in any ICO, you should exercise due diligence and conduct research.

How to Evaluate an Initial Coin Offering (ICO)

Initial Coin Offerings and cryptocurrency are emerging technologies, which means that the frameworks for assessing the value of ICOs and existing tokens are not available, yet. However, there are a handful of useful weighting systems that are being used to evaluate cryptocurrency

Initial Coin Offerings. Below are important questions worth keeping in mind when evaluating the potential of an ICO or cryptocurrency asset.

1. The Project

Does a centralized entity already offer the service? If, so why does de-centralization make it better?

Avoid projects that offer services or products that are already success-fully provided by centralized entities unless it makes existing solutions significantly different or better. A project with high potential is one which is not only disruptive but can stand out as a unique product.

What is the project's fiscal policy?

The fiscal policies of a project should promote the commercial benefit of its tokens for it to be attractive. There must be commercial benefits for token holders, such as having functionalities or rights attached to them. In that case, token utility lies in the services offered by the plat-form, and the market size—the more people that use the services and pay for it in the token, the higher the token value will be.

2. The Fundraising

What kinds of discounts are offered to early investors? How were the discounts determined? Do the discounts incentivize HODling or profit taking upon launch?

While discounts can be offered to incentivize investors to get involved early on, they should not be provided merely to encourage flipping or dumping. Only invest in projects that have real business models or seem feasible.

Does the project team provide any precautionary measures to ensure scammers will not be able to mislead investors into sending funds to the wrong address?

There have been issues with many ICOs falling prey to scammers who copy or fabricate an ICO's original website or communication channels to trick investors into sending funds to the wrong address. It is essential to check if the ICO in question has taken precautionary measures to ensure investors are directed towards the right address during the token sale.

3. The Team

Who is on the team, what are their background and credentials, and do they have any proven history or industry experience?

You need to conduct due diligence to ensure that the team behind the cryptocurrency has experience, has great industry expertise and contacts and that their LinkedIn profiles are verifiable. Remember you're not only investing in their products but also in the people running it.

What milestones does the project have in place? How will the team inform investors when milestones are achieved?

Only invest in an ICO that has a clearly defined roadmap with achievable and reasonable milestones along the way. Even so, the project must demonstrate that they're transparent and honest and that they can communicate their goals and achievements, and respond to queries and concerns effectively.

4. The Legal

Does the ICO fall within SEC jurisdiction?

Depending on where you live, ICOs are treated similar to security assets, in most cases. When evaluating an ICO, ensure you check if it complies with the U.S Security Exchange Commission (SEC) regulations as well as KYC or AML policies. Is the issue of regulatory compliance sufficiently addressed? If the project is not adhering to regulations, don't invest.

5. The Financials

What will be the use of the proceeds raised?

The total supply of tokens should be reasonable and justified based on the needs of the project. The distribution of the tokens after the public sale should be carefully planned and transparent. If the project is not clear on how the funds raised will be utilized, it is a red flag.

6. The Base Code

Where can I find the source code?

For credibility reasons and the sake of transparency, an ICO must make the source code freely available to the public to review. Not only is this more transparent, but the community can also inspect the protocol and suggest improvements to the code. Steer clear of projects that have non-existent base code or are close sourced.

How to Spot a Token That Will Rise in Value After an ICO

The best way to make money off of an ICO is to keep pace with what's going on in the industry. However, you may have to decide whether you want your investment to be a long-term or short-term investment.

If after purchasing an ICO you choose to hold the tokens for the long-term it is essential to assess the value of the token so you don't end up sitting on crypto that has no real worth.

Indeed, some coins continue to increase in value simply because the demand is high, but they may not have a long-term supported value. So how do you look out for such coins?

Supply and Demand

The first thing to consider is the token supply and demand. The token's value can only go up if there's an increase in its demand. Also, the token's supply has to stay the same or decrease.

The supply of the token you've just bought can be influenced in the following ways:

Token cap- If a cap or limit is on the amount of tokens available for circulation is set by the project team, the token value will go up with an increase in demand.

Token buy back- If the project team decides to buy up tokens that are in circulation and burn (destroy) the purchased tokens by using smart contracts, the value of the token will increase due to less supply.

Token creation- If the project team allows tokens to be mined or decides to create new tokens when necessary, the token supply increases resulting in a decrease in its value.

As mentioned in the previous sections, token demand is based on utility. Tokens that are used to pay for services within the project are more useful than the ones that are not attached to any functionality. If a token utility is based on the services delivered on the platform, the services offered must be enticing enough to generate high demand. The more people use the services and pay in the token, the higher the token value will be.

Market Size

The true worth of a token also is tied to the market that the ICO is appealing to. There are two techniques that traders use to judge the market size of ICOs.

Top-down market size - This is where an ICO defines the entire market without specifying their competitors. In this case, it is not a good strategy to determine the true value of ICO purely by the total market size. A good analyst will calculate how the project team will penetrate the market and how much of the market size they can capture.

Bottom-up market size- This is the best strategy for judging the worth of an ICO, as it projects the growth potential of the project based on current numbers. The only problem with the bottom-up strategy is that many ICOs do not even have a working prototype by the time they launch. Consequently, analysts often are left with the speculation of top-down market size as the only method for judging the project's potential.

So how do you know if ICO will rise in value after ICO?

The less risky ICO is the one that has disclosed their market size bottom-up, with a proof-of-concept or beta version of the project that is favorable to adoption. However, such projects are scarce in the ever-growing ICO marketplace.

The key to profitably investing in cryptocurrencies is to minimize your risks. Invest in due diligence by assessing tokens' supply and demand as well as their market size to gain insights into the actual value of services offered and the market served. However, keep in mind that cryptocurrencies are a crazy market; you run the risk of losing money. Only invest in what you can afford to lose.

Chapter 25

How to Invest in Crypto Profitably

When it comes to cryptocurrency investing, a lot of research and due diligence is genuinely needed. Given their volatility, you should be wary of investing in crypto. However, the high demand for cryptocurrencies make buying and holding the safest bets for higher returns.

To become a more profitable investor in cryptocurrency, you must first master investing skills. Having sufficient skills helps you to minimize mistakes so you can make more money off cryptocurrency.

Like every other investments asset, cryptocurrency investing has four key stages. Below are the four steps of profitable investing in crypto along with the discussion on what you must do to reach the next stage of profitability.

Stage 1: "Unconscious Incompetence"

As a beginner investor, you start at "unconscious incompetence" since you don't even know enough to know what you don't know. Because there's so much unknown, the risk of failure is high. If you invest in crypto while you are at this stage, you risk losing money or receiving inconsistent profits. To avoid making losses, you'll need to rely on the investment advice of others.

Stage 2: "Conscious Incompetence"

If you conduct a little research or perform due diligence on the cryptocurrency you want to invest in, you progress to the "conscious incompetence" stage. You've taken your first steps forward by saving and investing passively. However, you still lack active investing skills and risk management knowledge. If your portfolio losses and profits feel out of control or you don't even know why you're profitable sometimes, and unprofitable others, move to the next stage.

Step 3: "Conscious Competence"

You are at "conscious competence" when you know enough about the cryptocurrency investing game to get comfortable. Investing at this stage is marked by a solid investment plan and execution based on proven strategies that lead to success. However, you may occasionally experience undesirably large losses even though your portfolio has reasonable return characteristics. These losses occur because your particular investment approach isn't firmly grounded in risk management. To avoid these occasional blunders and losses, you must master the intricacies of profitable investment approaches.

Stage 4: "Unconscious Competence"

This is the final level of consistently profitable investing. An investor who is at this stage knows cryptocurrency so well it becomes their comfort zone. You don't invest based on advice offered by others, but seek their help for factual information. Further, your financial situation is no longer dependent on someone else – you're truly "financially independent." This stage is also marked by someone who has mastered risk management and investment strategies that create a consistently profitable portfolio through all market cycles.

Why Risk Management is Important

As an investor in crypto, you must aim for the highest level of profitable investing. The best way to advance to the next level is to master investment risk management. The wise investor plans on minimizing mistakes by strategically managing risk exposure.

When you carefully control your losses for each crypto investment, it reduces anxiety because you know that when mistakes occur, the damage will be contained.

Investment risk management allows you to move to the next stage of profitable cryptocurrency investing with confidence and peace of mind. It is the key to growing your returns on investments and achieving the financial security you desire.

How to Avoid Losing Cryptocurrency Investments Before They Cost You Money

Before making any investment in cryptocurrencies or ICOs, it is critical to perform due diligence. Investing without knowledge is expensive – what you don't know about crypto investing will cost you money.

In the cryptocurrency investing, the critical skill that separates professional investors from novices is due diligence. Profitable cryptocurrency investing requires due diligence, as it helps you to investigate all aspects of the cryptocurrency before putting your money on it.

Below are the first due diligence questions you must ask yourself before investing or trading cryptocurrency.

1. How can I lose money on this investment?

One thing about cryptocurrency investing is you don't understand the investment until you know all the ways you can lose money with it. The best way to analyze your investment is to identify in advance all significant risks that can lead to losses. Once these risks are adequately determined, the second step involves proactively managing whatever risks are controllable. With an objective investment strategy, you typically manage every significant proportion.

To ensure the preservation of your capital, ask if you can trust that particular cryptocurrency development team with your money. What is the background and history of each individual involved with the project? The truth is the team (ICO founders, advisors, and developers) is what matters most for any ICO. A stellar team with relevant industry experience and verifiable LinkedIn profiles is an indication of a higher potential for success. An unbalanced, weak and inexperienced team can be concerning.

2. How will this investment help me achieve my portfolio objectives?

For most investors who trade crypto, the portfolio objective is to maximize profit with minimal risk. To achieve this goal, you must consider spreading your investment over multiple coins by building a diversified portfolio.

Besides having a portfolio objective, you need to have a personal goal for investing that ensures you invest in crypto in a way that honors your values, interests, and tastes.

If you're considering putting money in cryptocurrency for long-term gains, then consider investing in projects that have the potential of enabling future growth. What that means is that you put your money in crypto that offers real-life use or has actual real technology behind it. A typical example of such coin is Ethereum, but there are other popular ones like Ripple, Bitcoin, IOTA, and so on. The key is to determine which coins have the inherent characteristics that best fit your interests, investment goals and risk tolerance.

3. What's my exit strategy?

You should always have an exit plan before investing in cryptocurrency. Regardless of which coins you acquire, no investment is appropriate forever. The cryptocurrency market is highly volatile, and market conditions change rapidly. When market conditions or your investment objectives change, it's time to exit without delay. It is important to set your exit plan in advance so that there will be no hesitation with the sell decision.

If you don't want to hold coins for extended periods and instead want to flip them for some short-term gains, make sure you set a plan along with your timeframe and exit price. A well-thought predefined exit plan helps to control losses when things go wrong. It also ensures you preserve your capital when the inevitable mistake arises so that you're prepared to invest in the next opportunity.

4. How does this investment make business sense?

Like any other investment asset, cryptocurrency investing must make business sense. That is, the valuation and return on investment must be congruent with the competitive advantage and barriers to entry possessed by the underlying business or project.

Because competition is critical for the growth of an ICO or blockchain project, you should assess if the ICO in question is focused on beating the competition. Has the ICO provided information on competitive analysis? Is there a significant demand for the project in question?

An ICO that offers above-market returns and excessive evaluations must provide a significant competitive advantage along with barriers to entry for future competitors to support its claims. Otherwise, the high yields and valuations will be watered down to the market level due to high competition. As a result, your investments lose money.

Further, some coins keeping increasing in value just because the demand is high, but they may not have a long-term supported value. This may not be sustainable and may soon turn out to be a get-rich-quick scheme. Look out for such coins.

In summary, you can avoid speculative bubbles that lead to losses if you apply common business sense when performing due diligence. If it doesn't make business sense, then it probably isn't real.

5. What are the price and token distribution structures of this investment?

Price analysis is crucial in assessing the worth of any cryptocurrency. An extremely low-priced token may send warning signals that the project is under-capitalized. Also, the total supply of tokens should be reasonable and justified based on the needs of the project. What percentage of tokens is allocated to founders, developers, and advisors? How will investors contribute their funds?

A good ICO campaign enlists the services of escrow agents to help with the supervision of the obligations imposed on the sale, and ensure that the funds are not released to the development team until the agreements of the set trade finalize. Escrow systems for ICOs are always facilitated by smart contracts to ensure trust and integrity.

Because the token's worth lies in the completion of the proposed milestones, a proper escrow states clearly the terms of the agreement so that breach of contract is avoided. Have they published the terms and conditions of the sale in clear language?

As an investor, you must carefully assess the escrow agents and the functions used in a particular token crowd sale before investing in such a token sale event. With ICO smart contracts, investors have a level of insurance and assurance that their funds are safe and will only be distributed after the completion of the said project. If the project fails to achieve the set objectives, the funds are returned to investors.

6. Has the project demonstrated early on that it can gauge the strength of the community to back its idea?

It is essential to check the cryptocurrency discussion boards to gain insights into the project's potential. BitcoinTalk is the most popular message board for cryptocurrencies. The forum allows people to come together to discuss and form opinions about crypto. It is also the best place to find the latest announcements about an ICO, ask questions with the developers of the coin and other members on the forum.

Use BitcoinTalk forum as well as Reddit and Twitter to research a coin. Check out the ICO's announcement thread. Are they responding to questions and concerns genuinely or are they vague and ineffective?

If the posts on a BitcoinTalk are too negative, read the thread carefully and do your own research to see if it's worth investing in that particular ICO. On the other hand, if a thread is too positive with no negative comments, double check the accounts to make sure they are credible. A team can trivially pay for bots and users to fabricate and post positive comments about their cryptocurrency.

Investing in the Long-Term

In the long run, buying and holding cryptocurrency is still the best strategy. It is not feasible at the moment to look at price charts every day because the gains you receive from day trading in crypto's change in value are minimal. Even if you don't make trading decisions based on these small changes, you still risk losing your investments if you make a terrible trade.

Another problem with investing in the short-term is that for technical analysis to be worth it, you'll need to put at least $50,000 in the market for it to be profitable. It is for these reasons that most investors opt for the buy and hold strategy. As already discussed in the previous section, always conduct due diligence before you invest in cryptocurrency, and only invest the money that you can afford to lose. With a robust portfolio objective and personal objective in place, you don't need to watch the price of your holdings every day like a hawk.

It is okay to check the market every day but do so without becoming emotionally invested in it. You can always check your investments and the market trends on a weekly, monthly and quarterly basis.

Finally, if your goal is to make quick bucks, consider short-term trading with margin. That means that instead of holding some coins forever, you simply flip them for some short-term gains. In short-term trading with margin, you take advantage of pre-announcements or airdrops to make quick bucks. This strategy works well with altcoins (any currency that uses same blockchain protocol as Bitcoin but is not a Bitcoin) or newly listed ICOs

Cryptocurrency Red Flags to Look Out For

The absence of regulations and a general lack of understanding of cryptocurrencies, in general, can cause confusion, creating a conducive environment for malicious characters to generate scam coins that serve to exploit the ill-informed. Don't be fooled.

Here are the most significant red flags that potential Ponzi schemes and scams use to help you know what not to invest in.

1. Huge returns that are unrealistic

If it sounds too good to be true, it probably is a scam. It's pretty standard to hear about investment opportunities in the crypto market that promises daily or monthly returns. The truth is no investment can consistently generate high returns with no risk or guaranteed returns whether it is a cryptocurrency, cloud mining or any other investment asset class.

A legitimate cryptocurrency does not raise funds based on the potential returns of your investment, but instead, they focus on their technology and goals. Steer clear of ICO campaigns that actively market the potential of their coins and not their technology or products.

2. Returns are highly dependent on referrals and new users

If it pays you out as long as there is a continuous supply of new users, it's a Ponzi scheme. If the pool of users dries up, the whole thing collapses, and you lose all your money.

A project that is legitimate does not need people to own its coin to grow. What it needs is the proper execution of their goals, excellent teamwork and useful technology. It's not your job to promote the project by getting more referrals to its coin.

3. Unclear or minimal information about on the founding team

A coin with minimal or no information about the team behind it is concerning. Even if the team information is provided, reverse image search photos of team members on Google. If you discover the image is fake or duplicated, avoid the project. Does the team have relevant industry experience and verifiable LinkedIn profiles?

Only invest in ICOs where the team is reputable, highly experienced in that particular industry, and respected by the community. It is not wise to contribute to projects that have anonymous developers or ghost team members.

4. You have to invest first to get more information

Many fraudulent schemes or scam coins pose as legitimate businesses such as Cloud Mining Services, Bitcoin Investment Packages (BIP) and Multi-Level Marketing platform. To get more information about the service, you have to either invest or sign up as a member to learn more. In fact, multi-level marketing schemes won't allow you to participate unless you click on their referral links. Some even use complicated buzzwords to confuse those interested to know how they are making the profits, to seem credible. Such schemes have a short life cycle and would shut down once there are little users left.

5. The non-existence of a code base

Given that blockchain and the majority of cryptocurrencies are open-source, projects that have closed-source code bases (code behind the coins is not released to the public) seem less credible. Legitimate projects have their source code freely available for the public to look and review via Github. The code can also be distributed and modified. A typical example of a transparent project is the Ethereum open source project.

The reason why scam coins do not reveal their code is that there is no code base at all.

6. The absence of key information

The lack of a whitepaper is a huge red flag. A whitepaper details all the information that you need to know about a particular cryptocurrency, from its purpose to its token economics and the way it works. Even if a whitepaper is provided but it is needlessly complex (too much jargon, complex English, vague explanations, etc.) be wary as it may hide the project's credibility by deliberately making the project hard to understand.

Conclusion

Congratulations you have made it to the end of this book! I believe you are now a better Bitcoin trader equipped with knowledge, strategies, and tricks to achieving optimal returns in your trades.

Remember, this book alone isn't all you need to become a better trader. You'll need to continue to grow, learn and adapt as your progress in your investment career. You should fully understand the features of any products or business projects you intend to fund, and carefully weigh the risks against the return before making a purchase.

Once again, thank you for purchasing this book. I hope that you were able to learn and master various Bitcoin and cryptocurrency concepts from this book that you can apply next time you go out to trade or invest in crypto.

Before you go, please take a moment and leave a 5-star review about this book on Amazon. In leaving a review, you will be able to help me continue to write the kind of books that get results. You will also assist in exposing this book to more people who can benefit a lot from it and become better cryptocurrency traders and investors. (Click here) to write a review for this book on Amazon. I highly appreciate it!

All the best as you set out on your investment journey. Thank you.

-- Michael Gonzalez

The Cryptocurrency Dictionary

Altcoin - Besides Bitcoin, there are literally thousands of other currencies that exist. These currencies, particularly newer or less popular currencies, are often referred to as "altcoins."

Arbitrage - The act of buying and selling on different exchanges to earn the difference in the spread. Arbitrage opportunities occur due to differences in exchange reputation, community coin preferences and ease of bank funding.

ATH - Stock traders might recognize this acronym, but tech enthusiasts may not. ATH is short for "all-time high," a place many cryptocurrencies have routinely visited in recent years.

Bag Holder - A term to refer to a trader who bought in at a high and missed his opportunity to sell, leaving him with worthless coins.

Bitcoin - Bitcoin was the first cryptocurrency created on the blockchain system back in 2009. It's decentralized and operates on a peer-to-peer network. It remains the largest and most valuable global cryptocurrency.

Block - A block is a group of cryptocurrency transactions that are grouped together and recorded on a blockchain after they have been verified. Once a block enters the blockchain, it is publicly available and permanent.

Blockchain - Blockchain is the underlying decentralized ledger that keeps cryptocurrency transactions secure. The blockchain is a public system of verifying cryptocurrency transactions using a peer-to-peer network of miners.

BTC - An abbreviation for Bitcoin. XBC is another popular abbreviation.

Circulating Supply - The price of a coin has no meaning on its own. However, the price of a coin, when multiplied by the circulating supply, gives the coin's market cap.

Coinbase - Coinbase is one of the largest and most popular cryptocurrency exchanges. Investors use the website and app to buy and sell cryptos and to monitor market prices.

Cold storage - Cold storage refers to storing cryptocurrency offline for security reasons. Coins held in cold storage are much more difficult for hackers to access, but it comes with its own set of risks if storage hardware is damaged, lost or stolen.

Cryptocurrency - A digital currency that runs on blockchain technology and a peer-to-peer verification system. Cryptocurrencies are decentralized and do not rely on banks or governments.

Cryptography - The art of writing and solving codes. Cryptography is used to protect cryptocurrency security and validate transactions.

Decentralized - In a decentralized system, no single source carries the critical data and record of transaction histories. Each device connected to a blockchain network has its own unique copy of the information stored on all the other nodes rather than a copy of the data stored on a central device, such as a server.

Fiat - While traditional government-backed currencies can undoubtedly be used to make digital transactions, crypto investors refer to these conventional currencies as "Fiat" money. Cryptos are decentralized, but Fiat currencies, such as the U.S. dollar and the Euro, and printed, managed and controlled by governments.

FOMO - FOMO, an acronym for "fear of missing out," can be applied to stocks as well, but some see FOMO as the real driving force behind the massive inflow of cash in the cryptocurrency market.

FUD- Short form of 'fear, uncertainty, and doubt.'

Hard fork - A hard fork is a significant change in the software of a particular currency that results in the splitting of its blockchain. Bitcoin Cash is a popular cryptocurrency that was created as a result of a hard fork in the original bitcoin blockchain.

Hash - A cryptographic hash is a mathematical function that takes a file and creates a code that can be used to quickly and easily identify the file. Each hash is unique and can't be reverse-engineered.

Hash rate - the Hash rate is a measure of how much computing power a cryptocurrency miner is generating. The higher the hash rate, the more powerful the mining machine.

HODL - HODL is a popular acronym in the crypto investing community which was initially just a misspelling of the term hold and now stands for "hold on for dear life." The term is a nod to the extreme volatility and unpredictable nature of cryptocurrency markets.

ICO - ICO stands for "initial coin offering" and is the crypto version of a newly-public company's initial public offering. ICO investors are hoping to get in on the ground floor of a new currency.

Ledger - A list of financial transactions for record-keeping purposes. The Bitcoin blockchain ledger is publicly available and cannot be altered.

Long- A position that a trader takes. To take a long position on something is to believe its value will rise in the future.

Market Cap - A stock's market cap refers to the market value of the company's outstanding shares. In the cryptocurrency market, the market cap is used to illustrate a coin's dominance in the entire cryptocurrency market.

Mining - Mining is the process by which people use advanced computers to process blockchain transactions. Because of how much time, power and expertise are required to process cryptocurrency transactions, mining rewards miners by paying them a small amount of cryptocurrency for their efforts.

Moon - A crypto slang that means such extreme bullish movement of a coin that it is heading to the Moon.

Node - Any computer connected to a currency's blockchain is referred to as a node. Each node maintains its own copy of the blockchain.

Open-Source - A software with publicly available code. Bitcoin is an open-source project.

Private key - A private key is a personal password to access a digital wallet. A digital wallet is only as secure as a user's private key is.

Public key - A wallet address is a hashed version of a public key which allows users to send cryptocurrency to your wallet. Private keys are mathematically related to cryptocurrency wallet addresses, but they are encrypted to prevent reverse engineering.

Pump and Dump- The recurring cycle of an altcoin spiking in price followed by a massive crash. Such movements are often attributed to low volume, hence the 'pump.' Traders who pump, buying huge quantities, may wish to invoke FOMO from the uninformed investors and then dump, or sell, their coins at a higher price.

Shill - The act of unsolicited endorsing of the coin in public. A trader who bought a coin has an interest in shilling the coin, in hopes of igniting the public's interest in that particular coin.

Short - A position that a trader takes. To take a short position on a coin is to believe its value will fall in the future.

Wallet - Hopefully everyone knows what a traditional wallet is, and a digital wallet works in a similar way. A digital wallet is simply a (hopefully) secure way for people to store their cryptocurrencies.

Whale - A colossal player who has a substantial amount of capital. Whales are often the market movers for small altcoins too due to their vast wealth.

Printed in Great Britain
by Amazon